Greenland

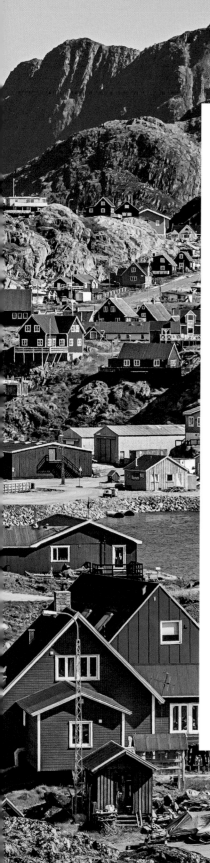

Frontispiece: **Sisimiut**

Consultant: Marianne Stenbaek, Professor of Cultural Studies,
McGill University, Montreal, Canada

Please note: All statistics are as up-to-date as possible at the time of publication.

Book production by The Design Lab

Library of Congress Cataloging-in-Publication Data
Names: Bjorklund, Ruth, author.
Title: Greenland / by Ruth Bjorklund.
Description: New York, NY : Children's Press, an imprint of Scholastic Inc.,
    2018. | Series: Enchantment of the world | Includes bibliographical
    references and index.
Identifiers: LCCN 2017054630 | ISBN 9780531130476 (library binding)
Subjects: LCSH: Greenland—Juvenile literature.
Classification: LCC G743 .B54 2018 | DDC 998/.2—dc23
LC record available at https://lccn.loc.gov/201705463

Scholastic Inc., 557 Broadway, New York, NY 10012

1 2 3 4 5 6 7 8 9 10 R 28 27 26 25 24 23 22 21 20 19

Greenland

BY RUTH BJORKLUND

Enchantment of the World™
Second Series

CHILDREN'S PRESS®

An Imprint of Scholastic Inc.

Contents

Left to right:

Humpback whale,
Sisimiut, colorful
houses, sled dogs,
traditional clothing

CHAPTER 1

Tradition and Change

MIKI AND HER GREAT-GRANDMOTHER SHARE A name. Miki's great-grandmother is gone now, but according to Inuit tradition, if parents give their newborn a deceased loved one's name, his or her spirit lives on. Even though people do not follow the naming custom as much anymore, Miki says she is proud to share her great-grandmother's name. Miki's great-grandmother lived in Qaanaaq, the northernmost village in Greenland. Many of Miki's relatives still live there and follow a traditional way of life. Most people make a living seal hunting.

Miki lives in a town called Aasiaat. Although Aasiaat and Qaanaaq are about 680 miles (1,100 kilometers) apart, they are not far from each other by Greenland standards. Greenland is the largest island in the world, more than three times the size of the U.S. state of Texas. Yet only about fifty-seven thousand

Opposite: **About 9 percent of the people in Greenland are over age sixty-five.**

people live there. Villages are far apart, and no roads connect them. For Miki and her family to visit relatives in Qaanaaq, they must travel by boat or airplane. They can only go by boat in summer, when the sea ice has broken up and there is open water. Fortunately, both towns have an airstrip.

Greenland is a very cold country. The northernmost part of Greenland is Kaffeklubben Island, only 440 miles (700 km) from the North Pole, the northernmost point on the globe. Most of Greenland is covered in a sheet of ice called the Greenland ice cap. Only the coastlines are free from ice. Consequently, that is where everyone lives. Although it is cold, there is not much snow in Aasiaat and even less in

Behind the Name

Despite its name, Greenland is anything but green. It is covered mostly in rock, ice, and snow. So why is it called Greenland? There are two theories. One dates to about a thousand years ago. At that time, northern European people known as Vikings explored and settled throughout the North Atlantic region. Erik the Red was a Viking who lived in Iceland. In about 980, he was exiled, or forced to leave, Iceland because he had committed murder. He went to the mostly unpopulated Greenland. When his exile ended, he did not want to return to Iceland. Instead, he wanted to encourage others to join him and establish a new Norse settlement. Because it would be difficult to lure people to a land composed only of rock, snow, and ice, he called his settlement Greenland. The second theory explaining Greenland's name is that the word is a mistranslation of *grund*, which in the Old Norse language means "ground."

Qaanaaq. The land is brown and rocky. It is dry year-round; northern Greenland is an Arctic desert.

Visiting Qaanaaq

Miki went to Qaanaaq the previous August to stay with relatives while her parents brought her brother to college. She loves summer. It feels so free to wear lightweight clothes and no gloves. The temperature barely goes above 50 degrees

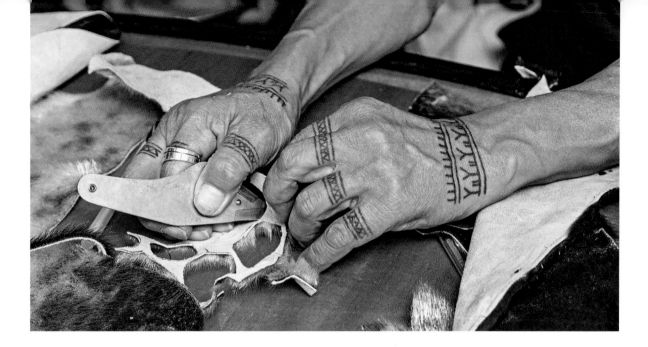

An Inuit woman demonstrates how to cut sealskin.

Fahrenheit (10 degrees Celsius), but to Miki, that feels warm. Being so far north, the sun barely sets in summer. It is light twenty-four hours a day. From April until August, the sky stays pink and orange most of the night—a never-ending sunset and sunrise. This can make it hard to fall asleep.

In Qaanaaq, Miki helped her aunts and cousins prepare clothing and food for fishing and seal-hunting trips. They mended and waterproofed parkas and anoraks. Miki helped repair her uncle's kamiks, which are sealskin boots lined with fur. It is not an easy task. Miki tried not to be frustrated by her lack of experience, especially while she watched her cousins, who had learned to sew in school. Most of the clothing was made in the traditional way, using seal and reindeer hide and musk ox fur. But modern waterproof fabrics were blended in to make the clothing lightweight.

In Greenland, the sea ice breaks up in August, clearing the way for boats. Traditionally, hunters used kayaks, but today most fishers and hunters have small motorboats. They hunt seals, mostly ringed and harp seals, as well as narwhals and halibut. Summer hunting and fishing is important for people in the village. They sell their abundant catch to seafood merchants from the south. Almost everyone earns most of their yearly income in August. In winter, it is too difficult for merchants to reach Qaanaaq.

One day, Miki's uncle was halibut fishing but not catching much. Suddenly, he spotted a breaching minke whale. Minkes are a kind of whale that native Greenlanders are allowed to catch. He was excited. He pulled out his cell phone and called

A humpback whale leaps from the water in Disko Bay, off the coast of Greenland. About fifteen different species of whales live near Greenland.

his cousins and friends. Soon, ten motorboats were following the whale. The hunters killed the animal quickly and dragged it to shore. They carved the whale in the traditional way, using knives they had made themselves. They divided the meat equally. Each stowed away some and brought the rest to fish markets in town.

Greenlanders also hunt in winter. Some men paddle kayaks and use hand-thrown harpoons to hunt seals, whales, and walruses. But most hunters cross the ice using snowmobiles or dogs and sledges (large, rugged sleds). One of Miki's uncles raises sled dogs. There are actually more dogs than people in Qaanaaq. In summer, Miki loved watching the young puppies' playful antics. But Greenland sled dogs are not pets. By the time they are nine months old, they are taught how to work.

In winter, hunters bring home seal, reindeer, walrus, musk ox, and sometimes polar bear. Nothing hunted is ever wasted. Miki's aunts and cousins freeze, salt, and dry the meat for food year-round. They can the blubber, the animal fat, to use for cooking. They use the hides for clothing and boots. Parkas, hoods, anoraks, and boots are lined with fur. People also make use of antlers, horns, and baleen, a toothlike material in some whales.

Life in Qaanaaq is much more traditional than in Aasiaat, Miki's hometown. Most residents of Qaanaaq are native Greenlanders, people who belong to the Inuit ethnic group. Tradition is strong in Qaanaaq but the village is changing. There are shops, a hotel, a community hall, a health clinic, a post office, and a new school. Everyone has electricity and cell phones and uses the internet.

Living in Aasiaat

Aasiaat is a town on an island in Disko Bay, off the west coast of Greenland. Disko Bay is dotted with islands and massive icebergs. Miki often sees whales from her bedroom window. The island is hilly, and brightly colored wooden houses sit high above the water. There are few roads in Aasiaat; almost no one has a car. People walk, ride mountain bikes, take boats, or use snowmobiles in winter. Aasiaat is Greenland's fifth-largest town, but fewer than 3,500 people live there.

Miki's father, Josef, moved to Aasiaat to go to school. Most villages have schools, but only a few towns have advanced high school classes. For several centuries, Greenland was a colony of Denmark, and Danish was the official language. Now, however, schools in Greenland teach students in the native Greenlandic language, Kalaallisut. Some schools also teach in Danish. When Miki's father came to Aasiaat, he studied Danish and English. He knew being able to speak three languages would help him get a good job.

A dogsled pulls tourists across the snowy land in Greenland. Sled dogs can travel at speeds of up to 20 miles (32 km) per hour.

Kayaks were invented by the Inuit people. Today, Greenlanders and tourists alike use kayaks to explore the waters.

After high school, Miki's father went to work for a tour company. He was well suited to the work. Besides his language skills, he also had traditional skills he learned growing up in a village. He was expert at kayaking and driving a dog sledge. Aasiaat is a growing tourist destination. In summer, Josef guides visitors on kayak trips, paddling around islands and icebergs. In winter, he takes tourists by dog sledge across the ice cap. Miki's mother, Eva, also works in the tourism industry. She is the curator of the town's museum. Aasiaat was settled during Greenland's early colonial period, in the 1700s. Many old colonial buildings remain. The museum is the former home of Knud Rasmussen, who explored the Arctic and recorded the stories of the Inuit people. The museum features colonial tools, modern Greenlandic paintings, and traditional Inuit arts and crafts.

College in Nuuk

Miki's brother has left Aasiaat and moved to Nuuk to attend the University of Greenland. He is studying environmental science. He plans to join scientists from around the world who come to Greenland to research climate change. Nuuk is the country's capital and the largest city, though only seventeen thousand people live there. Nuuk seems large and exciting to Miki. Her brother emails photos of the city's busy harbor and streets lined with shops, galleries, and cafés. There are cars, buses, and taxis. Miki is eager to go to college in Nuuk when she graduates from high school. Although she may move to Nuuk, or even to Denmark, Miki will always be deeply connected to the villages of her ancestors.

Women walk past a mural in Nuuk. About one out of every three people in Greenland lives in Nuuk.

CHAPTER 2

A Frozen Island

Greenland is the world's largest island. The land is covered by an ice cap and most of it is uninhabitable.

Greenland is geographically part of North America but politically part of Europe. Northern Greenland borders the Arctic Ocean. Greenland's nearest neighbor is Ellesmere Island to the northwest, which is part of the Canadian province of Nunavut. The two islands are separated by narrow, often ice-filled waterways called the Kennedy Channel, Nares Strait, and Smith Sound. Baffin Island, also part of Nunavut, lies to the west of Greenland. Between the two islands are Baffin Bay and the Davis Strait. Southern Greenland, bordered by the North Atlantic Ocean, is where most Greenlanders reside. Eastern Greenland has a rugged coastline facing the North Atlantic Ocean and the Greenland Sea. To the east across the

Opposite: **A boat approaches a towering iceberg off the coast of Greenland.**

Greenland's Geographic Features

Area: 836,330 square miles (2,166,085 sq km)

Area of Ice Cap: 656,000 square miles (1.7 million sq km)

Longest Fjord: Ittoqqortoormiit Fjord, 217 miles (350 km)

Highest Point: Gunnbjorn Fjeld, 12,119 feet (3,694 m) above sea level

Lowest Point: Sea level along the coast

Average Temperature in Winter: About 20°F (–7°C) in the south, –30°F (–34°C) in the north

Average Temperature in Summer: About 45°F (7°C) in the south, 40°F (4°C) in the north

Average Annual Precipitation: 10 to 30 inches (25 to 76 cm)

A man leaps over a crack in the ice near Ilulissat.

Ice in Balance

A healthy ice sheet is in balance. That means it has an equal amount of snowfall and evaporation. On an ice sheet, the heaviest snow falls on the ice dome. As the ice dome grows higher, glaciers spread downhill. In lower areas, the ice melts and evaporates. But when the ice sheet's balance is disturbed, glaciers either advance (grow larger from more snowfall) or retreat (pull back due to too much evaporation and snowmelt).

A glacier is always moving. As it moves, it carries rocky debris that it deposits along the ice flow. When the glacier flows rapidly, it forms deep cracks, called crevasses. In recent years, Greenland's glaciers have been retreating rapidly, forming wide swaths of crevasses.

Jakobshavn Glacier is Greenland's fastest-moving glacier. In 2012, it moved at speeds averaging 151 feet (46 meters) a day. This is three times the speed it moved in the 1990s.

Greenland Strait lies the European country of Iceland.

Three-quarters of Greenland lies above the Arctic Circle, the line of latitude that marks the area where at least for one day each year the sun does not completely set (June 21), nor completely rise (December 22). From north to south, Greenland extends about 1,660 miles (2,670 km). At its widest east to west, Greenland measures about 793 miles (1,276 km).

The Ice Sheet

Less than 20 percent of the land in Greenland is free from ice. Greenland contains one of the earth's two ice sheets, or ice caps, the other being in Antarctica. Together, these ice caps hold 99 percent of the world's fresh water. Greenland's ice cap is more than three times as large as the state of Texas. Some of the ice is more than 100,000 years old. An ice cap forms when snow falls but does not melt entirely. Layers of snow compress and form a dense mass of ice. Some parts of Greenland's ice cap are nearly 11,000 feet (3,350 meters) thick. If it melted, it would raise the level of the world's oceans 23 feet (7 m).

Greenland's ice sheet is the chief feature of the country's landscape. Throughout the interior of the country, the ice sheet is solid. The north central area contains the highest point, or

A scientist takes a snow sample at the Greenland Summit Station. Changes in the qualities of the snow reveal information about changes in the climate.

ice dome, of the ice sheet. There stands the Greenland Summit Station, a scientific research center, which monitors the ice cap and weather conditions. At the edges of the ice cap are large rock formations, glacial rivers bordered by moraines (rock deposits caused by moving ice, or glaciers), crevasses, and nunataks. Nunataks are the peaks of mountains not covered in ice or snow that pierce through the ice sheet. The highest mountain in Greenland is the Gunnbjorn Fjeld nunatak, which rises 12,119 feet (3,694 m) above sea level. Located in the Watkins Range in northeastern Greenland, Gunnbjorn Fjeld is also the highest mountain north of the Arctic Circle.

Nunataks rise above the surrounding snow cover.

Water

Much of Greenland's water is frozen, but there are a few rivers and lakes. Most rivers are on the west coast, but the longest river, the Borglum, is in the east. Greenland's riv-

In the summer, melting snow can create rushing creeks in Greenland.

ers are formed by melting ice and many flow to the sea underground. Likewise, many of Greenland's lakes lie under the ice sheet.

Sea ice is another form of water in Greenland. Sea ice is frozen seawater. Greenlanders take advantage of the solid sea ice to fish and to hunt. In northern Greenland, the sea ice remains almost year-round, essentially serving as land. Farther south, on the coasts, sections of the sea ice melt. Sea ice is shiny and it reflects the sun's rays back into the atmosphere. When rising temperatures of the ocean and atmosphere melt too much sea ice, less sunlight is reflected and more is absorbed. This creates a cycle that raises the earth's overall temperature.

Ocean currents affect Greenland's shores. The Transpolar Drift Current travels past northern Greenland, bringing sea ice

The midnight sun stays low in the sky, traveling around the horizon.

Land of the Midnight Sun

In winter, the region never experiences direct sunlight because of the angle of the earth toward the sun. The Arctic region is tilted away from the sun, causing northern Greenland to undergo months of darkness. Not until January 13, after several weeks of total darkness, does a sliver of sunlight appear on the horizon, and then only for fifty-one minutes. In summer, the Arctic is tilted toward the sun. Then, northern Greenland experiences constant sunlight, giving the region its nickname, Land of the Midnight Sun.

and icebergs. The East Greenland current is a frigid ice-filled current that prevents ships from traveling there. The warmer Gulf Stream passes by southern Greenland. When the Gulf Stream and the East Greenland Current meet, they churn vigorously and attract large numbers of fish that come to feed. The Gulf Stream passes up the west coast helping create slightly milder temperatures. Although icebergs float down from the north, Greenland's southwestern coast is generally ice-free.

Living on the Edge

Greenland's landscape varies only in its coastal regions. Northern Greenland, known as Peary Land, is arid. Little rain or snow falls there. The Arctic desert landscape is mostly barren rock with only occasional pockets of ice or snow.

The Northern Lights occur in many different colors, but the most common are green and pink.

Dancing Lights

In Greenland and other northern areas, winter skies produce light in the form of the aurora borealis, also called the Northern Lights. The lights are the result of electrically charged gases from the sun, which are attracted to the magnetism of the poles. When the sun's gases collide with the earth's atmosphere, blazes of bright color flash across the dark polar sky.

Eastern Greenland is extraordinarily remote. It is home to the ice cap, moraines, massive glaciers, the Watkins mountain range, and Gunnbjorn Fjeld. Immense fjords—narrow ocean inlets created by glaciers and bounded by steep cliffs—line the coastline. Ittoqqortoormiit Fjord is the longest in the world, at 217 miles (350 km). Tasiilaq, the largest community on the eastern coast of Greenland, rests along an iceberg-filled fjord. The town is home to a mere two thousand residents, mostly fishers and their families.

Much of Greenland's long coastline is dotted with islands. The largest of these is Qeqertarsuaq Island, which used to be known as Disko Island. It is located in western Greenland's iceberg-filled Disko Bay. Nearby is Uunartoq Island, which has

Greenland's National Park

The world's northernmost national park is Northeast Greenland National Park. The park, established in 1974, is also the world's largest by far. It encompasses about 45 percent of the land in Greenland. It is seventy-seven times larger than Yellowstone National Park in Wyoming. The park is in fact larger than most countries in the world. Only thirty countries are larger than it. The park features steep, rugged cliffs and mountains and spectacular fjords. Within the park's boundaries are also the ice dome, vast glaciers, and the mountainous desert region of Peary Land.

Rocky mountains in Northeast Greenland National Park

many hot spring pools. South of Disko Bay is Kangerlussuaq Fjord, which means "long fjord." The western coast is home to Eqi, Ilulissat, and Jakobshavn glaciers. The Jakobshavn Glacier is one of the most active in the world. It is one of the glaciers that carries Greenland's ice cap to the sea. As the glacier moves toward the Ilulissat Fjord, crevasses form. At some point, the crevasses split open, and with a loud boom, the glacier breaks off, or calves, an iceberg. The Jakobshavn Glacier calves more than 8 cubic miles (35 cu km) of ice each year.

Southwestern Greenland is home to most of Greenland's population. Most people live in Nuuk, the largest city. Southern Greenland's landscape is less extreme than other regions. It is home to mountains covered in vegetation, meadows, and

Urban Landscape

Nuuk is Greenland's largest city and its capital, with a population of 17,635. Greenland is a sparsely populated country. There are so few people spread across the region that its population density is 0 people per square mile.

Sisimiut, Greenland's second-largest city, is located on the west coast, about 200 miles (320 km) north of Nuuk. Its population is 5,483. People have lived in Sisimiut for more than 4,500 years. Inuit people were the first to settle there. In the 1720s, Danish settlers arrived. Today, the city has a mixed population of Inuit and northern European people. The city is growing fast. Its busy harbor is large enough to accommodate large cargo ships and cruise ships. The city is a regional center for education, including high schools that board students from remote areas and professional and vocational schools such as a branch of the Technical University of Denmark and the Greenland School of Minerals and Petroleum.

Fishing boats line the harbor in Ilulissat.

Brightly colored houses sit on the rocky shore of Sisimiut.

Ilulissat, with a population of 4,603 people, is located in northwestern Greenland, 100 miles (160 km) north of the Arctic Circle. The city sits on Ilulissat Fjord, the end of Jakobshavn Glacier. It is a lively city, with stores, restaurants, museums, and a bustling harbor and airport. Its tourist industry thrives as people from around the world come to see the fjord, the glacier, and icebergs.

Qaqortoq, home to 3,100 people, has Greenland's warmest climate. Located on a fjord in southwestern Greenland, it is surrounded by mountains, the sea, and Lake Tasersuaq. Its seaport and airport support the city as a tourist destination and major trading center. Many of Greenland's students attend high school and college in Qaqortoq.

farmland. Sheep graze on hillsides. Fjords indent the coastline, and icebergs farther north fill the horizon. Southern Greenland is the site of some of Greenland's European settlements. The southernmost tip of Greenland is Cape Farewell, or Nunap Isua.

Climate

Greenland has an Arctic climate. The most extreme weather conditions are in the north and interior of the country. There, temperatures in the winter average –31°F (–35° C). Summer temperatures can be somewhat milder, but rarely rise above

Icebergs that have broken off Jakobshavn glacier clog the water near Ilulissat. The word *Ilulissat* means "icebergs."

freezing for long. In the southern regions, the summer months' average temperature is 45°F (7°C), but highs in the southwest can reach 70°F (20°C) in July and August.

Arctic winds in the north are relatively mild, but hurricane-force windstorms can last for several days. The Arctic weather patterns produce little precipitation, especially in Peary Land. The eastern coast of Greenland receives the most snowfall and rough weather as fierce storms rip through the

Rugged, rocky mountains rise at Cape Farewell, the southernmost point in Greenland.

North Atlantic Ocean from Europe. Southwestern Greenland receives about 35 inches (90 centimeters) of precipitation each year, nearly all in the form of snow, while northwestern Greenland receives about 8 inches (20 cm) of snow annually.

Greenland's climate affects the rest of the world. Any major changes to glaciers or the amount of sea ice will affect ocean currents, temperatures, and the volume of the seas worldwide. Scientists have focused intently on Greenland in recent decades as they study how the melting ice from the world's rising global temperatures is influencing the rest of the world's climate.

Children play outside on a beautiful day in Ilimanaq, a village in western Greenland. Despite the sun, temperatures are cool. July, the warmest month, has an average daily high temperature of just 53°F (11.5°C).

CHAPTER 3

Arctic Survival

IT TAKES A STRONG ANIMAL AND A STURDY PLANT TO survive in Greenland's harsh Arctic climate. In spite of the challenges, many species of plants and animals thrive. Thousands of different species of plants and animals live in Greenland. Some live on land, while others are in the air or under ice. They live in forests, rivers, lakes, peat bogs, and the sea.

Opposite: **A walrus rests on an iceberg in the Arctic. A walrus's thick layer of fat helps it survive in temperatures as low as –31°F (–35°C).**

Hardy Plants

Greenland is home to many different species of plants. Where they grow depends on soil conditions. Most of Greenland's land is classified as tundra, meaning a treeless landscape with soil that is frozen all or most of the year. In most regions, trees are unable to send down roots, so only bushes such as heather, lingonberry, bilberry, rhododendron, thyme, and rosemary can take hold. But not all of Greenland's tundra has permanently frozen

White poppies are just one of the many types of wildflowers that emerge from Greenland's thin soil in the summer.

soil, called permafrost. In southern Greenland, the permafrost is about 10 to 36 inches (25 to 91 cm) below the surface. The upper layers of soil melt in summer, allowing larger plants to grow. Low-growing stands of birch, mountain ash, juniper, and willow form a small forest in the Qinngua Valley and along some south-facing hillsides, which receive the most sun. Although summer temperatures are cool in Greenland, the sun shines nearly twenty-four hours a day, helping wild-flowers and berry bushes thrive. Along the southern coast, the summer landscape is ablaze with colorful wildflowers such as primrose, cinquefoil, dandelion, angelica, anemone, rock cress, and arctic poppy.

Patches of moss and lichen are found throughout Greenland. They require very few nutrients and survive in Greenland's harshest environments. Mosses soak up water and enrich the soil. Lichens are plantlike organisms that come in colors like orange, brown, gray, green, and purple. They can grow in the Arctic north and provide large animals, such as reindeer, musk ox, and caribou, with food. Lichens are also part of the diet of humans living in the remote Arctic. Traditionally, lichens have also been used in medicine and fabric dyes.

In Greenland's milder regions, the summer sun melts the upper layers of soil. The melted snow cannot seep below the permafrost layers, so temporary marshes, ponds, puddles, and bogs form. These wetlands provide a place for plants to thrive. Animals take advantage of these watering holes to rear their young, build nests in the grasses, and feed on plants.

In autumn, some tundra plants turn deep red.

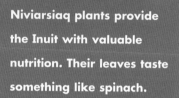

Niviarsiaq plants provide the Inuit with valuable nutrition. Their leaves taste something like spinach.

The National Flower

Greenland's national flower is the niviarsiaq, or dwarf fireweed. It is an herb that grows by watery areas where the snow has melted. The oval leaves have small pink or white petals.

After blooming, the flower forms a berry. The plant serves as food for animals and people. Humans eat the leaves raw, boiled, or made into tea. They also eat the flowers and the berries.

Animals and Their Adaptations

Greenland's animals have adapted to extreme weather and a stark landscape. Food is scarce. There is little vegetation, especially during the long winters. Shelter is hard to find since there are few forests, caves, meadows, or valleys. Yet animals make their home throughout the land.

Mammals

Large mammals that live in Greenland include musk ox, reindeer, polar bear, caribou, and Arctic wolf. Musk ox are native to north and northeast Greenland. They are the country's second-largest land mammal, standing about 4 feet (1.2 m) tall at the shoulder. Musk ox have thick woolly fur that hangs nearly to the ground. They have large hooves and both males and females have long, curving horns. Despite the name, they are not oxen, and despite their looks, they are not bison. They are more closely related to sheep and goats. In the summer breeding season, males fight over females. They charge toward each other and attack with their sharp horns and thick foreheads. During this ritual, the males give off a musky odor that gives them their name. Musk ox are herbivores—plant eaters. They use their hooves to dig into snow and scrape away ice to uncover vegetation.

The Greenlandic word for musk ox is _umimmak,_ meaning "long-bearded one."

The National Animal

Greenland's national animal is the polar bear. It is the largest land predator in the world. When standing on their hind legs, polar bears can rise as tall as 10 feet (3 m). They hunt marine mammals to survive. Polar bears live on Arctic sea ice throughout the year. They have a thick layer of fat and two layers of fur to keep them warm. They also have furry feet covered with small bumps to keep them from slipping on ice.

Polar bears have a strong sense of smell, which enables them to detect prey swimming under ice floes. Being so large, polar bears require a lot of food, mostly in the form of animal blubber, or fat. Adult males prefer to hunt for large seals, such as ice seals or bearded seals. Female and young polar bears hunt for smaller mammals, such as ringed seals. Polar bears also eat walruses.

Other bear species hibernate in winter, but polar bears stay active. However, they do go into a slower state known as walking hibernation, which helps them save energy and preserves their protective layers of fat.

Caribou, also called reindeer, are large elk-like animals that live in Greenland's Arctic north. They are known for their great migrations. Throughout the year, giant herds of caribou move hundreds of miles across the tundra in search of grasses, moss, and lichen. In winter, their hooves are sharp and

can cut through ice and snow. In summer, the hooves develop a spongy pad that helps them walk in mud. Both male and female caribou grow antlers, which they use to scrape moss and lichen off bushes, rocks, and ice. The strands of hair on caribou are hollow. This helps keep the animals warm in winter by trapping air inside the hair. Their hair also makes them buoyant, which is partly why they are strong swimmers.

Arctic wolves are powerful predators in Greenland. They hunt smaller animals such as foxes and hares. When hunting large animals such as caribou, Arctic wolves hunt in packs.

Arctic foxes prey mainly on small rodents called lemmings. They also raid birds' nests for eggs. The foxes store the

As caribou antlers grow, they are covered with a soft, velvety material that helps protect them. By the time the antlers fall off each year, the velvet has been rubbed off.

eggs in the permafrost. This preserves the eggs, providing the foxes with food all winter.

Arctic hares are the world's largest hares, standing about 2 feet tall (60 cm), not including the tail. They can run as fast as 40 miles per hour (64 kph). Arctic hares have short ears, which helps preserve warmth. Unlike other hares, Arctic hares do not make burrows because they cannot dig in the ice. Rather, they make nests of grasses. Arctic hares are a prey animal and must avoid attacks from polar bears, wolves, birds, and foxes. Their white fur camouflages them and their speed helps them run from danger.

Smaller mammals such as ermines, lemmings, and other rodents also make the tundra home. Lemmings, squirrels, and mice gather seeds, nuts, and bulbs and bury them in the ice for winter food. Ermines are vicious hunters that go after other small mammals, birds, and fish. They have thick, lush, white fur that was once prized for use in the robes of European royalty.

Sea Creatures

The seas of Greenland are abundant in marine life. Fish such as salmon, cod, halibut, rockfish, and sea trout inhabit the waters west and southwest of Greenland. These fish are especially fatty, helping them survive the cold.

Greenland's seas are home to an abundance of shrimp, crab, scallops, eels, sea worms, clams, and mussels. All grow slowly, especially snow crabs, which take almost ten years to mature. Scallops, found in the entrances to fjords, grow unusually large. Mussels are found clinging along rocky shores.

An Inuit man displays an Atlantic cod he just caught.

Greenland sharks eat fish and also scavenge whatever dead animals they find floating in the water.

Old-Timer Animal

The Greenland shark lives longer than any other vertebrate (animal with a backbone) on earth. Scientists estimate that Greenland sharks can live up to 400 years. The sharks do not reach adulthood until 150 years of age. Females are larger than males. Many grow 21 feet (6.5 m) long. They are nearly blind but have an extraordinary sense of smell. Greenland sharks are so powerful they can catch and devour a polar bear.

Greenland's Arctic waters are home to a variety of sharks and octopi. Most sharks are endothermic, meaning they can make their own body heat. Among them are blue sharks, salmon sharks, basking sharks, and the great white. Other species of sharks are cold-blooded, meaning they rely on body chemicals to keep from freezing. Several Arctic octopus species live in the deep waters off the northwest coast. The largest grow to 12 feet (3.6 m) across and weigh 160 pounds (70 kilograms).

Marine Mammals

Many species of whales live part of the year in the seas near Greenland. Many whales migrate south in winter to breed and raise their young. They return each summer and autumn to feed on krill, shrimp, sardines, and other creatures. Whales found off the Greenland coast include fin, sei, minke, sperm, humpback, beluga, orca, and the world's largest whale, the blue whale. Other less common whale species include bowhead and narwhal. Bowhead whales swim under the fast-flowing ice, and when they rise to breathe, they can smash through an ice floe 4 feet (1.2 m) thick. The narwhal is a toothed whale. The male narwhal has a massive tooth that protrudes from its snout and resembles a long tusk. Narwhals, prized by hunters for their "tusks," are some of the rarest whales in the world.

The narwhal's swordlike tooth can grow 10 feet (3 m) long.

More than two million seals live off the coast of Greenland. Seal species include ringed, spotted, hooded, bearded, and harp. Seals have four large flippers and are excellent swimmers, but when they move on land, they wriggle and bounce awkwardly. Most live in large groups. Ringed seals are the main prey of polar bears. Related to seals are sea lions, otters, and walruses. Walruses are huge and can weigh as much as a car. Both male and female walruses have tusks that grow 2 to 3 feet (60 to 90 cm) long. Walruses feed mostly on scallops, clams, and mussels. Although large and aggressive, they are prey for polar bears and orcas.

Birds

Many kinds of birds fill the skies in Greenland. Some remain year-round, and some stay only for mating season. Others stop over to feed or winter there, seeking refuge from colder Arctic climes.

The Arctic tern has the longest migration of any bird. It flies from the North Pole to the South Pole every year. Greenland is home to the world's smallest sea bird, the storm petrel, and its largest, the albatross, which has a wingspan of 11 feet (3.3 m). The ptarmigan, a chicken-like bird, is a year-round resident of Greenland. It lives everywhere—in meadows and wetlands, on rocky coasts and in the tundra.

Raptors found in Greenland include white-tailed eagles, ospreys, snowy owls, and gyrfalcons. The gyrfalcon is the largest falcon. It hunts along the coast and over the tundra. Snowy owls eat huge numbers of lemmings. An adult owl might eat more than 1,600 lemmings in a year.

Many ducks, puffins, and loons live in the ocean and summer wetlands. These waters are also home to wading birds such as herons, egrets, and spoonbills. Migrating birds that breed and raise their young in Greenland include snow geese, emperor geese, and tundra swans. In autumn, tundra swans migrate to the East Coast of the United States. They fly in large flocks at speeds of up to 85 miles per hour (135 kph).

Thousands of puffins nest along the coast of Greenland during spring and summer. In winter, they head south, where they spend months on the open ocean, diving for fish.

CHAPTER 4

Saga of the North

GREENLAND'S ENVIRONMENT HAS HAD A POWERFUL influence over the country's history. Thousands of years ago, people immigrated to the island and adapted to the challenging environment. Their skills and wisdom have been passed down through centuries. Northern Europeans first immigrated to Greenland about a thousand years ago. Their earliest historical records are found in long, written tales of adventure and achievement known as sagas.

Opposite: **Early people in Greenland made harpoons from the ivory tusks of walruses and seals.**

Ancient Beginnings

The last ice age ended about twelve thousand years ago. Around that time, most glaciers withdrew from Europe, North and South America, and Asia. But to this day, ancient ice sheets remain in Greenland and Antarctica.

Approximately 4,500 years ago, the first people migrated to

Greenland. They likely walked across frozen land from northeastern Canada. These people eventually disappeared, leaving little known traces of their culture. A few hundred years later, another group arrived. They belonged to what is known as the Saqqaq culture. The Saqqaq people lived in Greenland until about 800 BCE. Remains of their settlements are found along Disko Bay and the fjords near Nuuk. In these places, they could hunt abundant animals, including whales, harp seals, caribou, birds, and fish. The Saqqaq people made tools crafted from slate, quartz, wood, antler, and ivory. They made clothing from animal hides and fur. Some of their dwellings were large, built for multiple families, while others were small tents. The Saqqaq were also traders. This is known because many of their crafts and tools have been found in other Arctic regions.

The Dorset people migrated to Greenland around 800 BCE and survived until 1300 CE. They likely came from what are now northern Alaska and Canada. They lived on fish, birds, seals, and other marine life. Archaeologists have uncovered Dorset culture harpoons, knives, lanterns, and sculptures.

Europeans Arrive

After a long period of cool weather, Earth began to warm in about 900 CE. This era, called the Medieval Warm Period, lasted until about 1300. During this period, ice flows broke up and vast expanses of Arctic waters were exposed, enabling people to move about more freely.

Northern Europeans, called the Norse or Vikings, took advantage of the newly navigable waters and began exploring the North Atlantic region. Many Vikings settled in Iceland. Around 980, a Norwegian Viking named Erik Thorvaldsson, also known as Erik the Red, was banished from Iceland for committing murder. He had heard of a large uninhabited island due west of Iceland. So, in 982, he set sail and came ashore in southern Greenland. When his exile ended, he returned to Iceland to persuade others to join him. He assured people that the land was good for farming and raising livestock. In 985, he led a fleet of twenty-five ships, laden with goods, livestock, and settlers. Only fourteen ships and about four hundred settlers survived the voyage and landed near the tip of the southwestern coast, north of Cape Farewell. A short while later, more settlers arrived and established a smaller colony north of what today is Nuuk. The two settlements were known as the Eastern and Western settlements.

Viking explorer Erik Thorvaldsson was known as Erik the Red because of his red hair and beard.

The Medieval Warm Period served the Norse settlers well. Farms prospered from the warmer temperatures and the longer growing season. Meadows spread as the ice melted, providing pigs, sheep, and cattle with good grazing ground.

At their peak, about five thousand people lived in the Norse colonies in Greenland. They established about 275 farms, sixteen churches, two monasteries, and a cathedral. They built manor houses in the European style, with slate floors, large timber beams, and stained-glass windows. The Vikings traded Greenland's natural resources—furs, minerals, and walrus-tusk ivory to Norway and Iceland in exchange for building materials, tools, food, and household items. The Viking colonizers transplanted their European lifestyle successfully for a few hundred years, but ultimately, this lifestyle could not endure in the frozen north.

The Thule Culture

The effects of the warming period on the Arctic seas motivated other groups to explore. Inuit people, a people of the Thule culture living in the Arctic region, migrated rapidly through north-

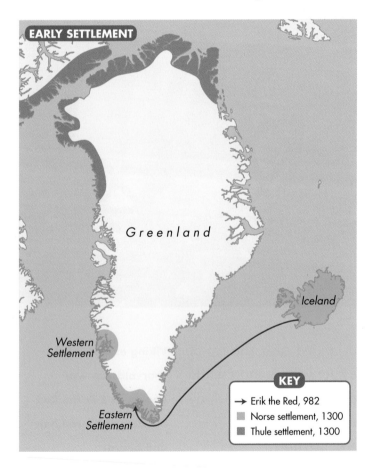

EARLY SETTLEMENT

Greenland

Iceland

Western Settlement

Eastern Settlement

KEY
→ Erik the Red, 982
Norse settlement, 1300
Thule settlement, 1300

ern Russia, Alaska, Arctic Canada, and Greenland. The melting sea ice opened new passageways that helped Thule fishers hunt large marine mammals such as walruses, bearded seals, and whales. They used harpoons to spear the animals, boats to hunt, and large drag floats to pull the animals out of

The Vikings made elaborate animal heads, which they sometimes placed on the prows of their ships.

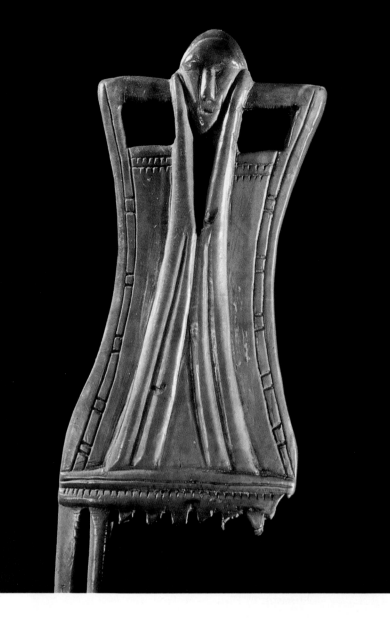

The Thule people made many kinds of objects from ivory and bone. This comb in the shape of a woman dates from about 1000 CE.

the water and across the ice. They carved bone and walrus-tusk ivory for decoration and made small amulets, possibly for help in hunting. Hunters used specialized harpoons to hunt for bowhead whales, which measure as much as 65 feet (20 m) in length. A single bowhead whale could feed an entire village all winter. On land, Thule hunters used lances and bows to hunt caribou, musk ox, and smaller mammals such as hares and foxes. The Thule were also the first people in the area to use dogs to pull their sleds, also called sledges.

With their hunting skills and the extra mobility dogsleds gave them, the people of the Thule culture settled widely in Greenland. They established communities and built permanent houses made with whale bones, stone, animal skin, and blocks of snow. Many were pit houses, built partially underground for insulation from the cold. They burned seal and whale oil in soapstone lamps for light and warmth. Thule communities constructed

Boys relax next to the large Greenland meteorite brought to New York.

Iron from Space

About ten thousand years ago, a giant meteorite fell to Earth. It landed in northern Greenland and split into many large fragments. The meteorite contained iron. The Dorset people used the iron from the meteorite to make tools. When people of the Thule culture arrived, they too saw the meteorite's usefulness. Some of the tools they made have been discovered as far away as Alaska. It was hard work getting the iron and fashioning spears, knives, and harpoons.

The native people were protective of their meteorite fragments. Many of the fragments were given names. At the end of the nineteenth century, American explorer Robert Peary took three massive pieces of the meteorite back home with him. Those three pieces, named the Tent, the Woman, and the Dog, are now on display in New York City at the American Museum of Natural History. The Tent is the largest meteorite on display anywhere in the world, and weighs more than 34 tons.

large storehouses to preserve their food. When on hunting expeditions, the people built temporary houses made of blocks of ice.

Contact

The Thule culture and the Norse settlers had relatively little contact. Each group followed their own ways and formed separate communities. For the most part, the Norse stayed in the south and farmed and raised livestock. The Thule fished and hunted in the northern regions. Not until the late twelfth century did the Thule people begin encountering the Norse. Most of the encounters were on the west coast. The Norse began moving north to hunt and fish. Norse sagas recount some violent skirmishes between the two groups, but not full-scale warfare. Many historians believe the groups engaged mostly in trade, rather than conflict. Remains of Thule settlements include Norse tools and implements. It is believed the Norse were not interested in learning about Thule tools and preferred to trade for food and clothing.

The Little Ice Age

Around the end of the thirteenth century, a volcano erupted in Indonesia on the other side of the world. It caused immediate global climate change. Volcanic ash and debris filled the atmosphere and deflected the sun's rays away from Earth, causing temperatures to drop and glaciers to advance. The onset of the Little Ice Age had a drastic effect on Greenland and its settlers.

As the cold settled in, the permafrost increased. Land suitable for farming and grazing shrank as the ice cap spread. Crops failed, and animals died off. The Norse had not learned the survival techniques of the Thule people, and as the climate

changed, they could not adapt. By the fifteenth century, the Norse settlements were completely abandoned.

Whalers and Missionaries

The descendants of the early Thule people of Greenland call themselves Kalaallit. For nearly two hundred years after the Vikings left, they were the sole residents of Greenland.

That began to change in the sixteenth century, when several European adventurers discovered Greenland's riches and saw trading opportunities. The English king sponsored Sir Martin Frobisher in 1578 to seek out the Northwest Passage, a hoped-for trade route west from Europe to Asia. Frobisher made a brief landfall near Disko Bay. A decade later, other English explored and mapped Greenland's west coast. By the

In Greenland, Thule people used boats called umiaks to travel around the coast. The boats were made of animal skins stretched across a wood or bone frame.

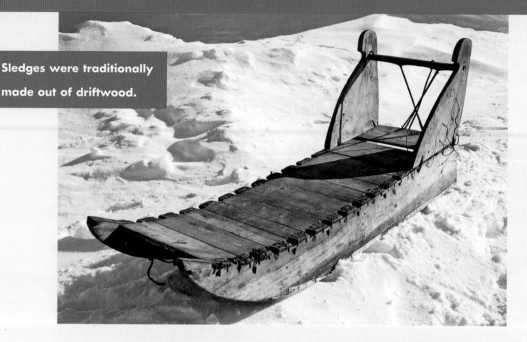

Sledges were traditionally made out of driftwood.

Getting Around the Arctic

Thule fishers and hunters invented methods of transportation that remain useful to this day. They made small, one-person boats called kayaks. Boatbuilders constructed a framework of driftwood or whalebone and covered it with animal skins. To make the boat watertight, they covered the seams with whale blubber. To use the kayak, a person fastened an animal skin "skirt" around the waist and attached it to the boat deck. This kept water out of the boat. The kayaks, propelled by a paddle with a blade at each end, were far more agile than any other type of boat. Thule boatbuilders also constructed larger, open boats called umiaks, to carry groups of people, goods, and dogs. They used walrus ribs to create the frame and covered the umiaks with walrus hide.

On land, fishers and hunters used sledges pulled by dogs. They built them using driftwood for the body and whale bones for the runners. Sealskins were cut and braided and used for the dog harnesses and reins. Sledge drivers wet the runners with water, which turned to ice, helping the sledge glide faster.

middle of the seventeenth century, Dutch, German, French, Basque, Danish, and Norwegian whalers plied the icy west coast in search of bowhead whales. They visited Kalaallit villages to trade for food and water.

Hans Egede and about forty colonists arrived in Greenland in 1721. They based their colony on Kangeq Island, which they called Island of Hope.

Permanent European settlement began in 1721, when a Norwegian missionary named Hans Egede convinced the Danish king to sponsor a mission to Greenland. Parts of Europe had undergone a major religious change called the Reformation and were now Protestant. Egede hoped to share the new religious teachings with any Norse survivors in Greenland. The king gave Egede and a group of merchants a charter establishing a trading company called the Bergen Greenland Company. The trading station was a failure and went bankrupt in just a few years. Although Egede found no Norse settlers to convert, he was successful in converting many Kalaallit people to Christianity. In 1728, he founded the village that is now the capital, Nuuk.

Egede was accidentally responsible for one of the worst episodes in Kalaallit history. In 1733, he took two Kalaallit children with him to Denmark for a celebration. The children became infected with smallpox. Upon their return, the smallpox spread from village to village, killing many people.

Two missionaries accompanied the children on their return voyage. They learned the Kalaallit language and set up missions throughout the southwest. Meanwhile, Jacob Severin, a wealthy merchant and friend of Egede, was assigned to oversee trade and Denmark's claim on Greenland. Severin successfully fended off threats from other Europeans, and strengthened Denmark's control of Greenland's natural resources and trade.

Greenland as a Colony

Unlike European colonizing efforts elsewhere in the world, the Danish colonization of Greenland was, for the most part, peaceful. The Kalaallit people had always survived the extreme environment because they believed in cooperation and communal living. They had no formal government or leaders. The closest leadership role was held by holy men. In 1776, the Danish government signed a charter authorizing the Royal Greenland Trading Company to manage trade, natural resources, and foreign relations. Denmark thus claimed Greenland.

For centuries, Denmark kept the Kalaallit people away from contact with the outside world. They controlled fishing rights and closed ports to all foreigners except those who had special permission. Danish merchants benefited from exclusive control of trade and natural resources. They bought whales and seals from Kalaallit hunters. The merchants made

An illustration from 1837 shows hunters approaching a bowhead whale. Bowheads were among the most common species hunted by European whalers.

Exploring Ultima Thule

Ultima Thule, a phrase used by the ancient Roman poet Virgil, means "beyond the borders of the known world." It is a name often used for northern Greenland. Beginning in the late nineteenth century, adventurers and explorers sought to unlock the secrets of the Arctic by trekking across Greenland.

Fridtjof Nansen

The first expedition across Greenland was led in 1888 by a Norwegian named Fridtjof Nansen. He spent a year learning from Kalaallit people on the northwest coast. Nansen skied for six weeks in the hope of reaching the North Pole. He never reached his goal. Later, he turned to humanitarian causes. He won the Nobel Peace Prize in 1922 for rescuing refugees and prisoners of war during World War I.

Knud Rasmussen

Knud Rasmussen, a Kalaallit/Danish explorer, was born in Ilulissat in 1879. He led his first sled dog team at age seven. In 1902, he began his first expedition, a two-year journey visiting Kalaallit villages and learning about Kalaallit culture. He published his travel journal, *The People of the Polar North*, in 1908. In 1910, he and explorer Peter Freuchen established the Thule Trading Station in Uummannaq. The Thule station became the base for seven major polar expeditions. In his most famous expedition, Rasmussen led his sled dog team 12,000 miles (20,000 km) across the frozen Arctic.

Peter and Mequpaluk Freuchen

Peter Freuchen cofounded the Thule station. Beginning in 1906, he sailed to northeastern Greenland to map the coastline. He then traveled by dogsled for more than 4,000 miles (6,500 km). He and his wife, Mequpaluk, made several explorations into the Arctic to study and record native culture. After Mequpaluk's death, Freuchen became an author and a filmmaker, documenting the lives of native Greenlanders and their island.

Knud Rasmussen and his sled dogs

Robert Peary and Matthew Henson

U.S. Navy admiral Robert Peary and his navigator, Matthew Henson, believed they were the first people of the modern age to reach the North Pole. The two established a base camp in northern Greenland, where they remained for more than a year. The camp included several Kalaallit families—women, men, and children—who assisted them in readying for the expedition. First by ship, and then by dogsled, Peary, Henson, twenty-two Kalaallit guides, and 130 dogs journeyed north. Henson arrived at the North Pole first, on April 6, 1909. Yet it was Peary who was honored by U.S. president Theodore Roosevelt for his accomplishment. Not until 2000 was Matthew Henson, an African American, honored for his achievement.

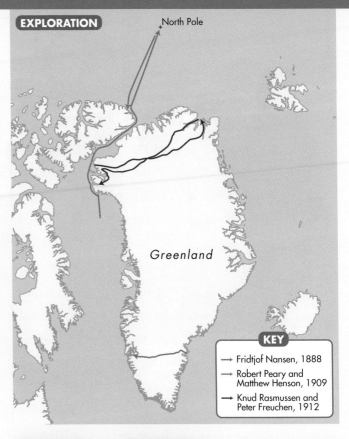

North Pole

Greenland

KEY
→ Fridtjof Nansen, 1888
→ Robert Peary and Matthew Henson, 1909
→ Knud Rasmussen and Peter Freuchen, 1912

Robert Peary dressed in fur clothing for his Arctic adventures.

Matthew Henson was already an experienced seaman when he began working with Robert Peary in 1887.

A Danish teacher poses with Inuit students in Greenland in 1915.

large profits selling seal oil and whale blubber to Europe for lamp fuel. Foreign access to Greenland's ports and waterways was not lifted until 1950.

Modern Greenland

Change came slowly to Greenland in the twentieth century. Kalaallit traditions continued to influence daily living for many Greenlanders. People of Danish descent lived mostly in Nuuk and other port towns. Not until 1940 did Greenland take a large jump forward.

World War II

On April 9, 1940, Germany invaded Denmark. With Denmark under German occupation, England, Canada, and the

Netherlands each wanted to annex Greenland. But the United States objected and entered into an agreement with Denmark. Under the agreement, the United States promised to protect Greenland against Germany and its allies in exchange for the right to build "landing fields, seaplane facilities, and radio and meteorological installations as may be necessary." The construction and operation of U.S. military bases brought sudden technological change to Greenland. Many people turned away from traditional lifestyles and entered the workforce as construction workers, miners, scientists, and technicians. Mining was critical. A cryolite mine in Ivigtut (now Ivittuut) supplied a key ingredient for aluminum production to use in building aircraft and boats. From 1941 to 1945, the United States built airfields and weather, radar, and radio stations; search and rescue bases; ports; and supply depots.

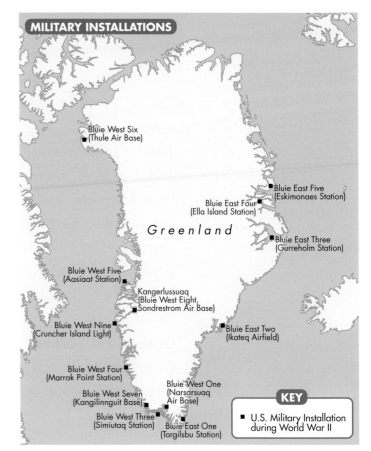

MILITARY INSTALLATIONS

Bluie West Six
(Thule Air Base)

Bluie East Five
(Eskimonaes Station)

Bluie East Four
(Ella Island Station)

Greenland

Bluie East Three
(Gurreholm Station)

Bluie West Five
(Aasiaat Station)

Kangerlussuaq
(Bluie West Eight,
Sondrestrom Air Base)

Bluie West Nine
(Cruncher Island Light)

Bluie East Two
(Ikateq Airfield)

Bluie West Four
(Marrak Point Station)

Bluie West One
(Narsarsuaq
Air Base)

Bluie West Seven
(Kangilinnguit Base)

KEY

Bluie West Three
(Simiutaq Station)

Bluie East One
(Torgilsbu Station)

■ U.S. Military Installation
during World War II

After the War

After World War II ended in 1945, many military installations in Greenland were abandoned. Some of the bases continued to function as defense and tracking stations. Some of the airfields were also used as refueling stations for flights between

Europe, Canada, and the United States. The largest airfields were Kangerlussuaq, Bluie East Two, and Thule Air Base. In 1991, Kangerlussuaq was sold to Greenland for one dollar. Today, it is an international transportation hub. The nearby harbor receives tourist cruise ships and scientific expedition vessels. Bluie East Two, on the remote northeast coast, was abandoned in 1947 leaving behind acres of rusting jeeps and airplanes, and leaking barrels of fuel. Thule Air Base continues to be a U.S. military base.

Greenland Today

Greenland today is a mix of ancient and modern. Cities support international trade, using modern port facilities and airfields. Some remote villages continue to survive following centuries-old traditions, while other villages are slowly emptying out, as people are lured by modern conveniences and the prospect of better jobs elsewhere.

Greenland is at the forefront of scientific activity investigating global climate change. World-renowned scientific research is taking place on Greenland's coast and ice cap. People in remote areas are gaining more access to technology. Homes have electricity and internet access. People use cell phones, ride tractors, and drive motorized boats.

Political and environmental conflicts are rising as Greenland struggles to achieve greater independence. In 1979, Greenland moved a step closer to independence when citizens voted for home rule, creating Greenland's legislature. In 2009, the Self-Government Act gave Greenland the right

to manage its justice system and to independently join international organizations.

To be completely independent, Greenland must support itself. But Greenland has high unemployment and relies heavily on benefits from the Danish government. By becoming independent, Greenland would lose much of that support.

Some citizens want increased development, especially in mining and fisheries. In 2013, Greenland's government, in a close vote, overturned a ban on uranium mining. Greenland has large deposits of uranium, rare earth elements, and other valuable minerals, and new mines will create jobs. People who live off the land, such as farmers and ranchers, believe their way of life and the clean environment are being threatened. As Greenland moves forward, the questions of economic development and independence will continue to be challenging.

Trucks and other goods rust away at the abandoned Bluie East Two military base.

CHAPTER 5

Law of
the Land

THE GOVERNMENT OF GREENLAND HAS EVOLVED
over time. Prior to colonization, Greenland had
no formal government. Native Greenlanders lived
in small settlements and worked their land in common.
Leadership was provided by senior family members or local
holy men. Then, in 1721, missionaries and traders arrived,
and Greenland was transformed into a Danish colony.

Opposite: **A young girl
helps a man vote at a
polling station in Nuuk.**

From Colony to Self Government

In 1953, the Danish government passed a constitutional
amendment changing the status of Greenland from a colony
to a Danish state. With the change, Greenlanders felt they
would receive more support from Denmark for education,
health care, and new jobs. But Danes still controlled government, business, and social institutions like schools. Many

A Look at the Capital

With a population of 17,635, Nuuk is Greenland's oldest, largest, and most bustling city. Colorful houses circle downtown's Old Town and busy harbor. Office and apartment buildings rise behind. Downtown Nuuk has shops, restaurants, and boutiques.

The city is Greenland's center of commerce. It has shopping malls, government offices, and business headquarters. It is also the country's cultural center. It is the home of the University of Greenland, the Greenland National Museum, and the Katuaq Cultural Center, which displays contemporary Greenlandic art.

A statue of Hans Egede looms over the city of Nuuk.

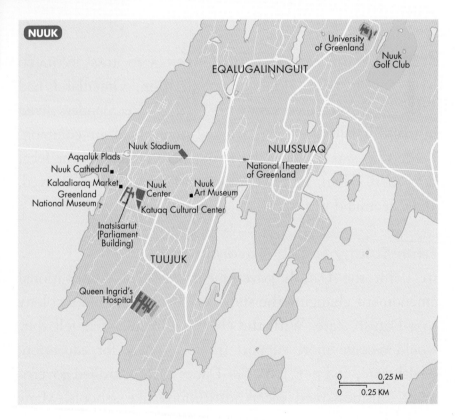

NUUK

University of Greenland
Nuuk Golf Club
EQALUGALINNGUIT
Nuuk Stadium
Aqqaluk Plads
Nuuk Cathedral
Kalaaliaraq Market
Greenland National Museum
Nuuk Center
Nuuk Art Museum
Katuaq Cultural Center
NUUSSUAQ
National Theater of Greenland
Inatsisartut (Parliament Building)
TUUJUK
Queen Ingrid's Hospital

0   0.25 MI
0   0.25 KM

Greenlanders felt the changes were not enough. In 1979, a majority of citizens voted for Home Rule. Home rule transferred legislative power from Denmark to a new Greenland legislature and gave native Greenlanders more say in their government.

After Home Rule, Greenland's fishing and mining industries expanded, but Denmark was still in charge of the operations and benefited most from the profits and trade. Many Greenlanders wanted local control of their fishing grounds and their mining operations. In 2008, three-quarters of Greenland's citizens voted in favor of the Self-Government Act, and on June 21, 2009, it went into effect. With self-government in place, Greenlanders have more control over mineral resources, legal matters, and the environment. The official language has changed from Danish to the native language, Kalaallisut, also called Greenlandic. Denmark continues to oversee defense, police, the courts, and currency.

Greenland prime minister Kim Kielsen (far right) signs an agreement affirming Greenland's commitment to the European Union, even as it has become increasingly independent from Denmark.

National Day

In 1983, Greenlanders selected June 21 to be National Day. Greenlanders celebrate National Day by gathering for speeches, parades, flag raising, and traditional skills competitions such as sled dog races. They enjoy holiday foods and drink while being entertained by musicians and folk dancers. June 21 is also a special day for Greenlanders because it is the date of the summer solstice, the longest day of the year.

A mother and child attend a celebration of Greenland's National Day.

Branches of Government

Greenland's government has three branches: executive, legislative, and judicial. The head of state is the Danish monarch, which is a hereditary title. The monarch appoints a representative to Greenland who is known as the high commissioner. The high commissioner has a seat in the legislature, or parliament. He or she can participate in legislative discussions of Greenland-Denmark affairs but is not allowed to vote.

Executive Branch

The executive branch is made up of the high commissioner, a premier (prime minister), and a cabinet of ministers. The premier is voted in by members of parliament. Typically, the premier is the leader of the party holding the most seats in the legislature. The premier selects cabinet ministers and proposes laws and budgets. Ministers oversee government departments such as finance, labor, education, health, environment, and fisheries.

Legislative Branch

Greenland's legislature is known as the Inatsisartut. It is a unicameral legislature, meaning that there is just one house. The Inatsisartut has thirty-one members who are directly elected by citizens to four-year terms. Any Greenlander age eighteen and older has the right to vote. Greenlanders also elect two representatives to the Danish parliament in Copenhagen, Denmark's capital.

The Greenland Parliament meets for two sessions a year, one in spring and one in fall.

Judicial Branch

The judicial branch of Greenland's government is made up of eighteen district courts, the Court of Greenland, and the High Court of Greenland. The Danish monarch appoints judges on the advice of a council of lawyers and judges. Judges are appointed for life or until they reach the retirement age of seventy. Lower court judges are not lawyers, but they are well-educated people highly knowledgeable of Greenlandic society. Higher court judges are lawyers. Appeals from lower courts are heard in the Court of Greenland. Further appeals progress to the High Court. On rare occasions, appeals cases may be brought before the Danish Supreme Court.

Greenland's Government

Monarch of Denmark

Executive Branch

High Commissioner

Premier

Cabinet

Legislative Branch

Parliament (31 members)

Judicial Branch

High Court of Greenland

Court of Greenland

District Courts

Political Parties

Greenland has several major political parties, which hold a wide variety of views on Greenland's relationship with Denmark. Siumut ("Forward") is a social democratic party that supports the present status of Greenland self-rule while remaining a part of the kingdom. Atassut ("Feeling of Community") is a more conservative party that believes in a strong relationship with Denmark. Inuit Ataqatigiit ("Community of the People") supports full independence from Denmark.

The government is slowly moving toward independence. In 2017, a new independence cabinet position was formed. The government is also making plans to draft the country's first constitution.

International Relations

Greenland is a member of the Arctic Council, an association of eight countries that fall within the Arctic Circle

Siumut supporters celebrate an electoral victory in Nuuk.

The Flag of Greenland

The flag of Greenland consists of a wide white stripe on the top and an equally wide red stripe on the bottom. The colors are the same as those found on the Denmark flag. Near the center of the Greenland flag is a circle. The upper half of the circle is red and it represents the sun setting. The lower half of the circle is white, representing snow and ice as well as the light that returns in the summer.

Greenland's flag was adopted in 1985.

and are devoted to environmental issues. Greenland is also a member of the Inuit Circumpolar Council, which advocates for the rights of native Inuit people living throughout the Arctic region.

On a larger international scale, Greenland is a member of the World Trade Organization (WTO). It is not, however, a full member of the European Union (EU) or the United Nations (UN). Greenland's delegates to the EU and the UN are part of Denmark's delegation.

Prime minister Kim Kielsen often wears a traditional Greenlandic coat called an anorak. It is considered as formal as a suit.

People in Nuuk celebrate Greenland's vote in favor of self-government.

"You, Our Ancient Land"

Greenland's national anthem is "*Nunarput utoqqarsuanngoravit*," or "You, Our Ancient Land." The words were written by Henning Jakob Henrik Lund, a Greenlandic writer, painter, and minister. The music is by Jonathan Petersen. The anthem was adopted in 1916.

Greenlandic lyrics

Nunarput, utoqqarsuanngoravit
Niaqqut ulissimavoq qiinik.
Qitornatit kissumiaannarpatit
Tunillugit sineriavit piinik.
Akullequtaasut merlertutut
Ilinni perortugut tamaani
Kalaallinik imminik taajumavugut
Niaqquit ataqqinartup saani.
Taqilluni naami atunngiveqaaq
Kalaallit siumut makigitsi.
Inuttut inuuneq pigiuminaqaaq
Saperasi isumaqaleritsi.

English translation

Our country, which has become so old
your head is all covered with white hair.
Always held us, your children, in your bosom
and gave us the riches of your coasts.
As middle children in the family
we blossomed here Kalaallit,
we want to call ourselves before
your proud and honorable head.
Humbleness is not the course,
Kalaallit wake up and be proud!
A dignified life is our goal;
courageously take a stand.

CHAPTER 6

Making Their Way

THE HISTORY OF GREENLAND IS A STRUGGLE OF SUR-vival in a harsh environment. Nearly every citizen has, or has had, relatives who lived in a subsistence lifestyle, having just enough food and money to stay alive. They hunted and fished to feed, clothe, and provide shelter for their families. They survived the hardships of an extreme climate and long days of near total darkness. Greenlanders in many rural communities continue to live this way. Today, people earn a living in a variety of ways—traditional, modern, and a blend of both.

Opposite: **An Inuit hunter lays traps to catch seals. Seal meat is an important part of the traditional Inuit diet.**

A Fishing Nation

Fishing is the largest industry in Greenland. Most fishing is done off the west coast. There are nearly nine hundred commercial fishing boats and more than five thousand smaller

In Greenland, halibut and other fish are sometimes hung to dry as a way to preserve them. Fish make up about 90 percent of Greenland's exports.

boats. Fishers catch about 80,000 tons of fish annually. The biggest catches are Atlantic cod and halibut. Because of warming seas, other species of fish not commonly found so far north are moving into Greenland's fishing grounds. These include Atlantic salmon. The chief types of shellfish harvested are snow crabs and shrimp. More than 40,000 tons of shrimp are caught each year. Newly discovered shrimping areas in northeastern Greenland produce particularly large shrimp, which are highly prized. The state-run fishery, Royal Greenland, is the world's largest supplier of wild shrimp. Other shellfish harvested are oysters, scallops, and mussels.

Most commercial fishing boats are generally based in bigger towns, where people onshore work to support the industry. They work in shipbuilding and repair, dock maintenance, gear manufacturing, food processing, and food storage. In offices, brokers organize the sale of the catch to retailers, wholesalers, and distributors. Other people provide services in law, trade, advertising, and safety.

Hunting

Traditionally, hunting for seal, whale, and other mammals was the most important source of income and nutrition for the native people of Greenland. Today, only about 10 percent of workers are involved in the hunting industry.

Seal hunting is a traditional source of income and livelihood for many Inuit families in remote locations. Seal meat is the chief food in their diet. The hunters and their families make use of all parts of the animal. The hides are used in clothing, constructing dogsleds, and making hunting equipment. Today, seal hunters in Greenland have quotas and must have licenses and be trained in humane hunting practices. International animal rights groups have called seal hunting inhumane. Most countries have passed bans on importing seal skin and fur. The hunters' income has dropped 90 percent since the bans took effect. The Greenlandic government argues that the seals are vital to the health and livelihood of villagers in remote regions. In 2016, seal hunters harvested 88,000 seals, mostly ringed and harp seals. Defenders of the Inuit people's traditional way of life point out that the seal population is robust. Denmark's foreign minister stated, "Seals are hunted in a very sustainable way. The meat is eaten by the Greenlanders and the fur is sold. That's as sustainable as it gets."

A farmer works in a
potato field in southern
Greenland. Potatoes
are among the most
common crops grown
on the island.

Whale hunting is controlled by the International Whaling Commission (IWC). The IWC is responsible for conserving whale populations throughout the world. In 1986, the IWC banned all whaling with only a few exceptions. The IWC allows native whaling societies, such as the Inuit, to hunt. Every year, it grants each group a quota. Greenland's Inuit hunters must have professional licenses and hunting gear designed to be the most humane. In Greenland, whale products are distributed around the country. No whale products are exported. Whale hunters earn very little—their boats and

equipment are expensive. Most of the benefit for hunters and their families is the meat. Profits are used to maintain their boats and gear. Greenland whalers hunt beluga, narwhal, minke, and porpoise whales.

Greenlandic hunters also hunt other animals. Reindeer are the most hunted large animal. In 2016, hunters harvested about 11,000 reindeer, 2,000 musk ox, and 140 polar bears. But hunting as a livelihood is getting more difficult. The climate is getting warmer and melting the sea ice. When the water does not freeze, or does not freeze thick enough, hunters on their sleds and snowmobiles cannot travel across the ice to hunt.

Bird hunting is another traditional occupation. Sought-after bird species include guillemot, eider, auk, ptarmigan, and goose.

Agriculture

Less than 1 percent of land in Greenland is suitable for farming. Few agricultural products are grown, and none are on a large scale. Only south Greenland is warm enough in summer to raise fruits and vegetables. However, as the climate warms, farmers have gained an extra two weeks of growing time. While that is good news, summers are now much drier and farmers must collect and store rainwater or build costly irrigation systems. Many crops are covered in tarps overnight to protect them from frost. Historically, the Vikings grew barley and potatoes. Modern farmers are establishing cool-weather crops beyond potatoes, such as onions, broccoli, cauliflower, spinach, celery, beets, turnips, carrots, and berries.

City-dwelling and town-dwelling Greenlanders are eating less meat and want more fruits and vegetables in their diet. The government is helping farmers experiment with new crops and construct commercial greenhouses. If the country is to achieve independence, officials say, it must produce more food locally and not rely on expensive imported foods.

What Greenland Grows, Makes, and Mines

Agriculture (2016)

Sheep	17,000 animals
Reindeer	3,000 animals

Manufacturing (2016)

Fish processing	80,000 tons
Shellfish processing	44,500 tons
Hides and skins	$300,000 in exports

Mining

Gold	4 tons
Quartz	182,000 tons

About 15 percent of Greenlanders are employed in agriculture, and most of them raise livestock. Sheep raising is the largest activity. Sheep graze along fjords, where the steep hillsides and rocky shores provide natural fencing. The southern fjord region supports about seventeen thousand sheep. But farmers there face serious challenges in trying to grow enough

hay to last the winter. There are also about three thousand domesticated reindeer on small farms. Poultry and dairy production is limited. There are fewer than two hundred cows or chickens in the entire country. To improve these numbers, the government is developing programs to help more people raise dairy cows, bees for honey, and ducks, geese, and chickens for meat and eggs.

A barge carries sheep across a fjord in Greenland. In Greenland, most sheep are raised for meat.

Mining

Beneath Greenland's ice and rock lie vast reserves of iron, aluminum, nickel, zinc, gold, rubies, and sapphires. But few mines are in operation. A small ruby mine near Aappaluttoq opened in 2017, and it is hoped that a gold-quartz mine in Isua will provide 4 tons of gold per year.

Foreign mining companies have been given licenses to explore Greenland's minerals. Explorations near the southern

Mining in Greenland is expected to grow as global warming exposes more rock where valuable minerals lie.

towns of Narsaq and Kvanefjeld led to the discovery of the world's second-largest deposit of rare earth minerals. Rare earth minerals are used in smartphones, hybrid cars, wind turbines, computers, televisions, and other electronics. Mining these minerals, however, is controversial. At the proposed mining sites, more than 100 million tons of rare earth minerals lie embedded alongside a huge deposit of radioactive uranium. To extract the rare earth minerals, the uranium must also be extracted. Greenland's government has lifted a long-standing ban on uranium mining. Communities near the mine fear that farmland and the environment will be damaged. However, many mining experts and economists believe rare earth minerals and uranium mining will provide enough income for Greenland to become an independent nation.

Tourism and Other Services

Greenland's two largest industries are fishing and hunting. Fishing has seen steady growth, but hunting has decreased. Unemployment hovers around 9 to 10 percent. Many people leave their communities to seek work in the bigger towns of Nuuk, Ilulissat, and Sisimiut.

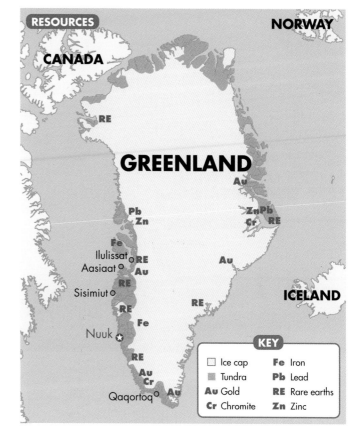

People who move to these towns find jobs in service industries. They work as bus or taxi drivers, construction workers, and dock workers. Some find jobs in restaurants, hotels, and retail shops. The bigger towns, especially Nuuk, are experiencing a building boom. New, modern apartment and office buildings are filling more of the skyline. Cruise ships and other large ships are coming into port, and harbors are being updated to accommodate them. While some villages are emptying out and abandoning their airports, larger towns are improving their transportation facilities.

Tourism is slowly becoming important as Greenland's economy changes. Ilulissat, the city bordering the Ilulissat Icefjord, is developing rapidly. About thirty thousand to forty thousand tourists visit Greenland each year. They want to see glaciers, icebergs, the northern lights, whales, sled dogs, and Greenland's native culture. Many subsistence hunters and

A cruise ships passes in front of an iceberg near Ilulissat. Roughly twenty-four thousand people travel to Greenland on cruise ships every year.

fishers work as guides for visiting sport fishers and hunters. Likewise, many artisans make livings selling traditional clothing, jewelry, beadwork, and carvings to tourists. Towns and settlements near tourist attractions are opening new hotels and restaurants.

Many Greenlanders who do not work in tourism work in other service industries. They include teachers, bankers, lawyers, shopkeepers, and health care workers.

Communication, Transportation, and Energy

Although Greenland is far removed from Denmark and the rest of Europe, modern communication technology brings it near. Even in remote regions, buildings have satellite dishes to provide cell phone service and internet connections. Two underwater high-speed communications cables connect

Money Facts

Greenland does not have its own currency. The country uses the Danish krone (kroner is plural). Each krone is divided into one hundred ore. Coins are minted in 50-ore, and 1-, 2-, 5-, 10-, and 20-kroner denominations. Paper currency is printed in denominations of 50, 100, 200, 500, and 1,000 kroner.

Danish bills and coins

Kroner banknotes are printed in many colors. The 1,000-kroner note is red. On the front is an image of the Great Belt Bridge, a bridge-and-tunnel link across Denmark's Great Belt strait. On the reverse is an image of the Trundholm Sun Chariot statue. This artifact, which was discovered in Denmark, dates to about 1400 BCE.

In 2018, 1 krone equaled $0.16, and $1.00 equaled 6.27 kroner.

Greenland to Canada and Iceland. Nearly four-fifths of the population are internet users. The Greenland Broadcasting Company broadcasts public television and radio to many communities. Danish colonists published the first national newspaper in 1861. Today, the national newspaper, *Sermitsiaq*, is widely read in print and online. It is published in Kalaallisut, Danish, and English.

Transportation is difficult in Greenland. Few roads connect towns. In fact, there are only about 100 miles (160 km) of roadway in the entire country and only about 40 miles (64 km) of them are paved. Many roads are passable only in summer. Generally, only city and town dwellers own cars or trucks. Elsewhere, people travel by bicycle and snowmobile, and in remote areas, by dogsled. Long-distance transportation is by

The Greenland Dog

The Greenland dog is a long-haired, muscular dog used as a sled dog throughout the Arctic. The breed first came to Greenland from Siberia four thousand years ago. The Thule people were the first to train these animals to pull their sledges across the ice. Today, the people still rely on sled dogs to transport hunters and carry food, medicine, and supplies to remote settlements.

The dog is suited to the cold climate. It has a short, furry inner coat and a medium-long, waterproof outer coat. In a storm, sled dogs bury themselves in snow, which insulates them from the cold.

Greenland dogs are rugged, and there are laws to keep the breed pure. No other dog breed is allowed above the Arctic Circle, and if a Greenland dog is taken below the Arctic Circle, it cannot return.

Puppies begin training at nine months. Inuit mushers—dog sledge drivers—train several dogs and select the strongest and the smartest to pull their sleds. Training a sled dog team requires great skill, patience, and knowledge.

Greenland has the largest population of sled dogs in the Arctic. However, their numbers are decreasing. Twenty years ago, there were about twenty thousand. Today, there is only about half that. One reason is that fewer people are hunting, so they need fewer dogs. Dog food is also expensive. Many mushers have turned to snowmobiles for transportation. Nevertheless, the Greenland sled dog remains a vital part of Greenland's economy and lifestyle.

boat or airplane. Air travel is important. Most of Greenland's imported food comes from Denmark. Large jets laden with goods land at the former U.S. military base in Kangerlussuaq. From there, the food is loaded onto smaller airplanes and helicopters to distribute to outlying settlements.

Greenland is dependent on oil for nearly all its energy needs. The country imports all of its oil and jet fuel. However, hydropower plants have been built recently, fulfilling some of the country's electrical needs.

Since Greenland has few roads, airplanes are often the quickest way to get around the frozen land.

CHAPTER 7

The Greenlanders

ONLY ABOUT FIFTY-SEVEN THOUSAND PEOPLE LIVE in Greenland. More than four-fifths of Greenland's population lives in the southwest. The rest of the population lives in small settlements in the north and east between the edges of the ice cap and the sea. Communities are generally far apart and no roads link them.

Ethnic Groups

Around 1000 CE, the Inuit people of the Thule culture migrated across coastal Alaska and Canada and settled on the coasts of Greenland. Present-day Inuit Greenlanders are the descendants of the Thule people. They call themselves Kalaallit ("the People"), or simply Greenlander.

Today, Kalaallit are the majority of the people in Greenland. Approximately 88 percent of Greenlanders are either Inuit or

Opposite: **Greenlanders dressed in their national costume, a colorful mix of animal skins, European cloth, and beads.**

Population of Major Cities (2017 est.):	
Nuuk	17,635
Sisimiut	5,483
Ilulissat	4,603
Qaqortoq	3,100
Aasiaat	3,010

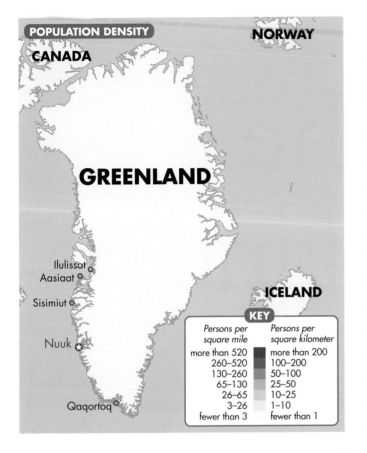

NORWAY

CANADA

GREENLAND

Ilulissat
Aasiaat

Sisimiut

ICELAND

KEY

Persons per square mile	Persons per square kilometer
more than 520	more than 200
260–520	100–200
130–260	50–100
65–130	25–50
26–65	10–25
3–26	1–10
fewer than 3	fewer than 1

Nuuk

Qaqortoq

Population by Ethnicity

Inuit
(Greenlander)   88%

Danish   11%

Other (Icelandic,
German, Norwegian,
Filipino, Swedish,
and Thai)   1%

Inuit people with mixed ethnic backgrounds.

In the tenth century, northern Europeans colonized part of southern Greenland, but they abandoned their settlements by the early fifteenth century. It was not until the early eighteenth century that Danish missionaries and traders began establishing churches and trading posts and founded Nuuk, the capital of the colony. Since that time, Denmark has kept its claim to Greenland. But Danish immigration has never been high. Only 11 percent of Greenlanders are Danish. People who make up the remaining 1 percent of Greenland's population have come from Iceland, Germany, Norway, the Philippines, Sweden, and Thailand.

Language

Since the eighteenth century, Denmark controlled the government and most of Greenland's commerce, education, foreign affairs, and trade. As a result, Danish, and not Kalaallisut (the West Greenland Inuit language), was the official language. In 2009, however, with the passing of the Self-Government Act, Kalaallisut became Greenland's official language. Kalaallisut

is also called Greenlandic. Two other Inuit languages are also spoken in Greenland. East Greenlandic has about three thousand speakers, and Northern Greenlandic has about one thousand speakers.

Inuit people throughout Greenland can speak and write Kalaallisut, and many, especially in towns, also know Danish as their second language. Most Danish people live in Nuuk, and many speak both Kalaallisut and Danish. More than seven thousand Kalaallisut-speaking people live in Denmark or in other European countries.

The first Kalaallisut-Danish dictionary was published in 1750 by Paul Egede, the son of the first Danish missionary in Greenland. In 1760, he published a Kalaallisut grammar book. In 1973, an official guide to phonetic spelling was published.

A sign in the Greenlandic language on a shop selling seafood

Common Phrases in Greenland

English	Greenlandic	Danish
Hi!	*Aluu!*	*Hej!*
How are you?	*Qanoq ippit?*	*Hvordan har du/de det?*
I am well.	*Ajunngilanga*	*Jeg har det fint, tak.*
Good-bye	*Ajungginniarna*	*Farvel*
Please	*Ikinngutinnersumik*	*Hvis du vil vaere sa venlig at*
Thank you	*Qujanarsuaq*	*Mange tak*

In Kalaallisut, each letter is pronounced separately, including double letters. Greenlandic words are often long. Syllables are added to a base word to express subject, possession, tense, or a description. Translated into other languages, such as Danish or English, Greenlandic words become phrases or sentences. For example, the English translation of the Greenlandic word *qimmeqarpunga* is "I have a dog."

Education

When the Self-Government Act named Kalaallisut the official language, all primary and secondary schools were required to teach students in Kalaallisut. Danish is taught as a second language, and sometimes English is taught as a third. All children are expected to attend ten years of school, from age six to sixteen. However, nearly half of all students do not go on to upper levels of education. There are eighty-five schools in Greenland, and each requires teachers who speak Greenlandic and Danish. It is not easy to hire teachers for rural schools. Some remote schools have as few as ten students. For some

rural students, the government offers online, long-distance classes. Some students choose to move to a bigger town to take advanced high school classes.

Students who want to continue on to college can attend the University of Greenland in Nuuk. Danish is the language used in higher education because there is a shortage of professors who are bilingual and a lack of textbooks available in Greenlandic. Many students leave Greenland to attend college in Denmark, and many choose to not return.

Greenland has a literacy rate of 100 percent, meaning all citizens over the age of fifteen can read and write their language. Greenland has a strong history of literacy dating to the colonial period when Danish missionaries taught the Inuit people written language. Books and newspapers have been available there since the early nineteenth century.

Children at a school in southern Greenland. About one in five Greenlanders is under age fifteen.

CHAPTER 8

Traditions of Faith

RADITIONALLY, INUIT GREENLANDERS FELT A SPIRItual bond to the animals around them. Their traditional beliefs gave way to Christianity when Europeans arrived. Today, nearly all Greenlanders follow the Christian religion, but they also continue to feel a deep connection to animals and nature.

Opposite: **In Greenland, the rituals of spiritual leaders called shamans often include drumming and dancing.**

Animism

Traditionally, the Inuit of Greenland believed objects and living things possessed an inner spirit, or *inua*. They also believed the inua affected all the events around them. The only way to survive their harsh environment was to respect nature, animals, objects, and each other. People took pride in themselves and believed in the power of their own spirits. Yet when facing difficult challenges, they turned to a familiar, or helping

spirit. The spirit could help in the hunt, or prevent sickness or misfortune. The spirit was represented by an object such as an owl claw, a polar bear tooth, or a piece of seal hide, which a person would wear.

Rituals and Taboos

The Inuit people lived by a moral code that included rituals to follow and taboos to avoid. A good, healthy life and a successful hunt depended on obeying the code. Life was communal and everyone in the village played a role in the hunt. Hunters showed respect for the animals they hunted. They performed songs while paddling their boats, and they always hunted using freshly cleaned weapons. After the hunt, they sang and danced to thank the animal's spirit. The first large animal killed in the hunt was shared equally throughout the community.

The people believed that whenever misfortune occurred, be it sickness, bad weather, or an unsuccessful hunt, it was due to evil spirits. The evil spirits attacked because some person or group had disobeyed a taboo. Such taboos included eating land and sea animals on the same day; sewing clothes of caribou hide while hunters were seal hunting; or hunting marine animals with weapons previously used to hunt land animals. (It was necessary to smoke weapons over a fire of seaweed to clean them.) When taboos were broken and misfortune fell upon someone, people sought help from a shaman, or *angakok.*

The Angakok

The angakok could be either a man or a woman, although it was usually a man. Children of angakoks often learned the secret customs from their fathers or mothers. A young person who showed unusual strength and sensitivity could be chosen for training, even if he or she was not a shaman's child. Angakoks learned special songs, stories, dances, drumming, and rituals. They performed ceremonies to heal the sick, bless the village, and pray for successful hunts. The angakoks wore ceremonial clothing and masks to increase their powers. The masks were often carved to look like dogs, as dogs represented journeys. People believed that the angakoks could foresee the future, interpret dreams, and journey to the spirit worlds of the sky and ocean.

When people turned to an angakok for help, the angakok went to the spirit world to look for answers. After returning, he or she would ask if a taboo had been broken. To calm the

spirits, the angakok might recommend offering gifts to the spirits or suggest that the guilty party move away. Often, the angakok assigned unpleasant tasks or charged a fine. Severe punishment was very rare. In serious situations, the angakok carved bone figures of monsters, called *tupilaqs*. The tupilaqs were sent out to sea to destroy evil spirits. The fear, however, was that an evil spirit would be more powerful and could send the tupilaq back, bringing even more misfortune. When an angakok completed an act of healing, he or she returned to normal life in the village until called upon again.

Marriage, Birth, and Death

In traditional Inuit society, men married as soon as they could support a family. When young women became old enough to bear children and marry, they received tattoos on their faces. The painful tattoo ritual prepared young women to be strong. Most tattoos were images of animals, whose spirits guided and protected them.

Greenlandic shamans sometimes covered their faces with masks during rituals.

In birth rituals, the angakok performed a blessing ceremony. A woman and her newborn had to live alone in a separate house or tent for one month if the baby was a boy, and two months if it was a girl. Parents named their children after a dead relative in the belief the relative's spirit would live on.

People believed that humans were made of three parts: a body, a spirit, and a name. When a person died, only the body was gone, and the spirit lived on in the child who bore his or her name. At death, the body was often buried where it had been born. Men were buried with weapons and tools, facing north, toward the hunting grounds. Women were buried with cooking pots, jewelry, and sewing needles. Both women and children were buried facing south, for warmth. Family members wrapped the bodies with soft carpets to carry them into the spirit world. People mourned their dead for five days, and at the end, a ceremony was held and then everyone returned to daily living. It was believed some people's spirits went to the sky and others into the ocean.

The tradition of tattooing dates back thousands of years among the Inuit people. Ancient mummies discovered in the ice show evidence of tattoos.

According to Norse mythology, Thor wielded a hammer and rode in a chariot pulled by goats.

Enter Christianity

The first Europeans who migrated to Greenland believed in many gods. These included Frigg, the goddess of love and marriage, and Thor, the god of war. People practiced their faith privately, offering gifts to individual gods during times of need. Norse mythology described a varied afterlife. The spirits of persons who lived an exceptionally good life were lifted to a heaven called Asgard. The spirits of the wicked went to an underground teeming with snakes and dripping

Historic Churches

Greenland's first Christian church was built around 1000 CE, at the request of Tjodhilde, the wife of Erik the Red. It was located in Qassiarsuk, and was also the first church built in North America. The Norse Christians built sixteen churches and a convent. Hvalsey Church was the first cathedral and its ruins still stand. Made of stone, the cathedral rests on a fjord in present-day Qaqortoq. The last known written record of Norse settlement—a notice of a wedding in 1408—was found there.

After the arrival of Danish missionaries, many more churches and chapels were built. One of the northernmost churches in the world, Zion's Church, is located in Ilulissat on Disko Bay, more than 200 miles (320 km) north of the Arctic Circle. Devout Ilulissat residents had written to the Danish king in 1777, requesting a church. At a cost of 157 barrels of whale blubber and 59 whale skeletons, the church was built and opened in 1782. Zion's Church is the oldest church in Greenland that is still used as a church.

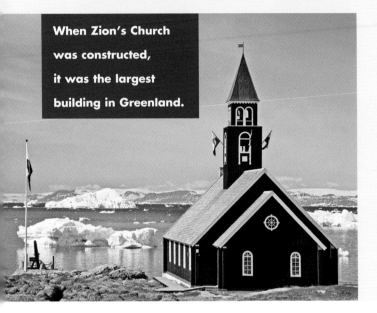

When Zion's Church was constructed, it was the largest building in Greenland.

poison. Courageous Vikings joined the gods in a spirit world called Valhalla, and the spirits of most everyone else went to a dreamlike world called Hel. By the beginning of the eleventh century, however, Christianity gained influence over the Norse, and their belief in multiple gods faded.

Christianity is the religious faith of those who believe Jesus Christ is the son of God. At the end of the tenth century, Erik the Red's son, Leif Eriksson, arrived in Greenland, bringing two priests sent by the Norwegian king. By the time the Norse left Greenland in the 1400s, most people had converted to Christianity.

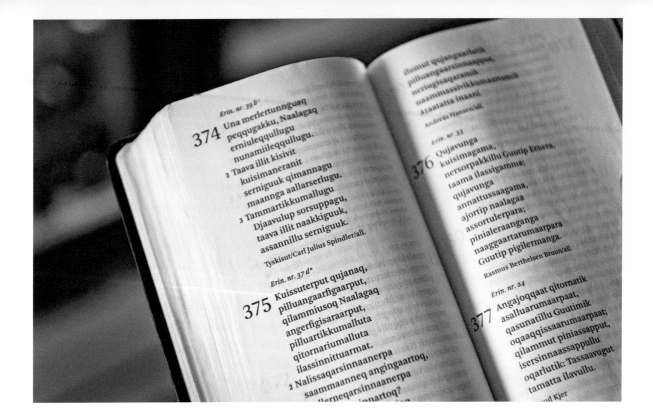

A Bible in the Greenlandic language

Religion in Greenland

Lutheran	96%
Traditional	1%
Other	3%

(including no religion, Baptist, Mormon, Jehovah's Witness, Roman Catholic, and Seventh-day Adventist)

At this time, all Christians in Europe were Roman Catholic, a church led by the pope. Then, in the sixteenth century, Europe underwent a religious change called the Reformation. During the Reformation, church reformers, called Protestants, questioned the pope's power and authority. They believed religious teaching and authority should belong to rulers and pastors. The Reformation inspired the Danish king to spread these new teachings across his kingdom. He sponsored a mission to Greenland, led by Hans Egede, who converted the Inuit people. Egede was hampered by his inability to speak the language, but he converted many people through pictures and deeds. His son, Paul, grew up in Greenland, knew the native Greenlandic language, and translated the Christian Bible into that language.

The Bishop of Greenland

The leader of the Church of Denmark in Greenland is called the bishop of Greenland. Today, the person holding that title is Sofie Petersen. She comes from a religious family. Her father was also a pastor. Petersen studied religion in Copenhagen, and then she returned to Nuuk as a Lutheran minister. In 1995, she became the first Inuit woman to be ordained a bishop in the Danish Lutheran Church. She is active regarding the issue of climate change because it affects the lives of Greenlanders. Also, she has overseen the publication of new Kalaallisut translations of Lutheran prayer books, hymnals, and the Bible.

Sofie Petersen was thirty-nine years old when she became the bishop of Greenland.

The new religion, Protestantism, included a variety of sects. The king of Denmark declared Lutheran Protestantism the official religion of the country. Small churches and missions were built along Greenland's coasts. By the end of the eighteenth century, nearly all native Greenlanders had become Protestant. Not until 1953 were Greenlanders allowed freedom of religion.

Today, Lutheran Protestantism remains the official religion of Greenland. It is practiced by more than 95 percent of the population. A small number of people continue to follow traditional Inuit beliefs. A few people in Greenland follow other religious faiths, including Baptist, Jesus Christ of Latter-day Saints (Mormon), Roman Catholic, Jehovah's Witness, and Seventh-day Adventist.

CHAPTER 9

Art of the Arctic

T HE EARLIEST ART IN GREENLAND WAS RELIGIOUS and ceremonial. More than two thousand years ago, people began decorating weapons, household items, and tools. They decorated harpoons, knives, clothing, jewelry, blankets, and even their skin. Greenland's long tradition of creativity continues to inspire artists to this day.

Early Art

Greenland's tradition of art dates to prehistoric times. Archaeologists have uncovered masks, carvings, and sculptures preserved in the ice. Some masks were made of animal hide and painted with bright natural dyes. Others were carved in bone, horn, and driftwood. Human hair was used for eyebrows and mustaches, and some were decorated with stones and feathers. Mask makers also created works with faces of

Opposite: **Traditional Inuit boots from western Greenland are made from sealskin. Dyed sealskin is cut into small pieces and then arranged into beautiful designs. The boots are often also decorated with embroidery.**

animals such as bears or wolves. Some masks were as small as 2 inches (5 cm) and were worn on the hands and fingers. Other masks were large, almost 2 feet (60 cm) high. Angakoks wore these when they danced during rituals.

Drums, made of wood and animal skin, were an important item for angakoks. They believed chanting and drumming lifted the angakok into the spirit world. Archaeologists have found remains of drums belonging to the Saqqaq culture, people who lived more than four thousand years ago.

The Greenlandic tupilaq is a special art form. Tupilaqs are carvings possessed of great power. Angakoks created them to destroy evil spirits. They made them using animal parts—bone, tusk ivory, antler, skin, hair, horn, and sinew. The figures were monsterlike with fearsome expressions. Angakoks carved them in secret, often away from the village and sometimes underneath a carpet or blanket. Once carved, the angakok breathed life into the tupilaq by performing special rituals.

A tupilaq figure from eastern Greenland

When European missionaries arrived in Greenland, they wanted to abolish tupilaqs, saying they were the work of the devil. The native people refused. When the missionaries insisted, the native people, though not the angakoks, began carving non-magical reproductions. A unique artistic tradition was born and continues to this day. Throughout the world, Greenlandic tupilaq figures are prized by museums and collectors.

Arts and Crafts

As the Greenlandic culture advanced, the people expanded into other artistic forms, making amulets, jewelry, beadwork, knitted items, and embroidery. Amulets carved from small pieces of wood, ivory, horn, or bone were worn as spirit guides. Women wore necklaces made of animal sinew and pendants carved in ivory, horn, and bone. They made iron tools used for mining a pink stone called reindeer's blood, light-blue lapis lazuli, and a clear green stone called *gronlanditten*. The stones were used in jewelry and knife handles. The designs were especially elaborate on the handles of a woman's knife, called an *ulu*.

Many artisans today follow the traditions of early Inuit designs and craftsmanship. Shops in towns and villages offer carvings, tupilaqs, masks, sculptures, amulets, knives, tools, pendants, earrings, beadwork, boots, and clothing. The crafts are produced using traditional materials such as bone, ivory, wood, hides, soapstone, antler, horn, and musk ox wool. Modern artisans are creating traditional designs with a contemporary flair and using newer materials such as silver,

An elderly Greenlander wears traditional beaded jewelry.

gold, ceramic, glass, and plastic. Tourists buy the carvings as mementos of their visit to Greenland.

However, not all of these beautiful crafts can be taken out of the country. An international organization called Convention on International Trade in Endangered Species of Wild Fauna and Flora (CITES) will not allow the trade of endangered species. In Greenland, tourists must have a special CITES permit to bring home items crafted from narwhals and beluga and minke whales, as well as walruses (such as an ivory tusk carving) and polar bears (such as a bear's tooth necklace). CITES forbids trade of items composed of parts from sperm, bowhead, fin, and humpback whales and all birds of prey. Crafts made from seal, reindeer, and musk ox are allowed.

Toys

Inuit people made toys for their children. They were crafted in fine detail. They made small kayaks that were perfect replicas of large ones using sealskin, sinew, bone, and wood. They also made small dolls, carving them from wood, bone, and ivory. The dolls' clothing was realistic, with sealskin parkas, gloves, and boots adorned with fur. Some dolls were dressed in ceremonial clothing. The dresses and blouses were brightly colored, beaded, and embroidered. The dolls wore tall, sealskin boots decorated with musk ox fur and embroidery. Although these toys were beautiful, they were more than playthings. The artisans used such detail as a way of teaching children how things should look and how things should be done.

Traditional Inuit dolls

Greenland on Display

Museums and galleries feature Greenland's artists, artisans, and incredible natural history. The Greenland National Museum in Nuuk has priceless artifacts on display, including ancient umiaks, tupilaqs, amulets, and prehistoric tools. An exhibit also includes four mummies dating back to 1475. They were among seven mummies found by hikers in 1972. Being frozen in the ice, the mummies are perfectly preserved. Their clothing is nearly intact. The women's tattoo lines can still be seen on their faces. The museum also exhibits traditional and modern arts and crafts.

A visitor looks at a display at the Ilulissat Museum.

The Ilulissat Museum

In northwest Greenland sits the Ilulissat Museum, the childhood home of explorer and social scientist Knud Rasmussen. The museum features a blend of old and new. There are exhibits of ancient artifacts and contemporary artists. The home itself is an exhibit displaying the traditional Inuit lifestyle of the nineteenth century. The museum exhibits clothing, tools, household items, and photographs taken by Rasmussen when he interviewed Inuit people living in the far north. There are also contemporary photographs, paintings, and displays describing melting ice and how it affects people today.

The Nuuk Art Museum features figurines made of bone, horn, and soapstone as well as paintings by Greenlandic artists. The Katuaq Cultural Center in Nuuk exhibits contemporary local artists such as Aage Gitz-Johansen and Aka Hoegh. The architecture of the building is also notable. It has colored, waving walls and rooflines inspired by the Northern Lights. Besides works of current artists, the Qaqortoq Museum in southern Greenland features displays of the Norse, Thule, and Dorset cultures. The Tasiilaq gallery in eastern Greenland has a large collection of arts and crafts, including tupilaqs and amulets made by the country's leading Inuit artisans.

Music and Dance

As contemporary Greenlandic art often reflects art from the past, so does Greenlandic music and dance. Dancing was performed by angakoks as ritual and by people in ceremonies and celebrations. Drummers usually accompanied dancers. The dances told stories, and the dancers wore masks that represented people, animals, plants, ice, and everyday items. Mask dances were performed for religious purposes, entertainment, and to teach children about life. A theater group in the 1970s revived the forgotten art of drumming and mask dancing.

The Katuaq Cultural Center hosts concerts, movie screenings, and conferences in addition to art exhibits. It is the most notable piece of modern architecture in all of Greenland.

The group interviewed elders and studied writings. Today, traditional dances, with modern variations, are performed in theaters and meeting halls throughout the country.

Inuit women have a song tradition called throat singing. It is a competition between two people, so the singer who lasts the longest is the winner. One singer begins and then is joined by the second person. Singers make sounds that are part of real life, such as ice cracking or babies crying.

Traditionally, drummers also performed in competitions, but not good-naturedly. Rather, a drumming competition was held between two men who had a dispute they could not resolve. When drumming, the men insulted each other until the most injured party left the competition.

Greenland is also the home of modern musicians, such as the hip-hop group Nuuk Posse, who rap in English, Danish, and Kalaallisut, and rock bands Chilly Friday and Small Time Giants. Greenland has also produced pop singers like Angu

Motzfeldt, whose music has appeared on European music charts, and Julie Berthelsen, who has performed before Danish royalty. Several classical music composers blend traditional Greenlandic music with classical elements, including Mads Lumholdt with his orchestra Nowhereland, and Adrian Vernon Fish, whose symphonies are inspired by Greenland's landscape.

Telling Stories

The oldest form of Greenlandic literature is storytelling. Large groups would gather and listen to the elders tell stories of cre-

Greenlanders take part in a drumming competition in Qaanaaq, in northwestern Greenland.

Portraying Greenland

Writer and artist Hans Lynge was a figure of major importance in the Greenlandic art world. His life spanned most of the twentieth century, and throughout his long career he depicted his country in his works as an author, painter, sculptor, printmaker, and playwright.

Among his many works are paintings and sculptures that depict people such as national heroes and Inuit women with children; impressionistic paintings of Greenlandic myths and landscapes; and several books and screenplays depicting life in Nuuk. A school and cultural center in Nuuk has been named in his honor.

ation, disaster, and courageous feats. Many of the tales have been preserved by the telling and retelling through generations. Modern authors have written books with similar themes of adventure and the spirit world.

The National Theater of Greenland produces plays with traditional and modern Greenlandic themes. Besides plays, the theater group also performs mask dancing, singing, and modern and traditional dance.

Filmmaking is a growing art form in Greenland. Documentaries depict Inuit life and the effect of climate change on Greenland. These include *Village at the End of the World*. The award-winning fictional film *Inuk* has similar themes. In it, filmmaker Mike Magidson tells the story of a teenage boy from Nuuk who dreams of becoming a rock star. His parents are unable to take care of him and he is sent into foster care in the north, where he is apprenticed to a seal hunter. There, he learns about the hardships of survival on Greenland's ice cap and the importance of melting ice on the villagers' way of life.

Inuk was praised for its stunning visuals. It showed at film festivals around the world.

CHAPTER 10

Strong Communities

FAMILY AND COMMUNITY ARE AT THE HEART OF Greenland's way of life. In the rugged climate of the north, people must rely on one another. Families, groups, and villages have always owned land in common and shared responsibilities. They hunt, fish, build homes, and raise children together. Hivshu Ua, the Greenlandic great-grandson of naval explorer Robert Peary, says, "We have family relationships stronger than in Western countries, because in this area we have to survive, and family members are important for survival, and we keep it that way."

Opposite: **All-terrain vehicles are useful for getting around remote villages.**

Towns and Settlements

Life in rural areas remains traditional. Hunting, especially seal hunting, and fishing are the norm. The entire community participates. Rural communities are small, ranging from a few

dozen to a few thousand residents. Most villages have a meeting hall, small stores, a chapel, a post office, a health clinic, and schools. Some have an airplane landing strip. Permanent houses are made of wood and painted bright colors. Temporary houses, for use while hunting, are made from snow, driftwood, canvas, and rock. Roads are few, people travel by boat, dogsled, snowmobile, and air. Other than hunting, there are few employment opportunities.

Nuuk and other bigger towns are fishing ports. When commercial fishing technology improved, more advanced fish processing factories were built. The factories lured workers from rural communities. New job opportunities also opened in tourism and mining. At first, it was mostly the women who moved away, leaving the men at home to hunt for walrus, whale, and seal. But many young people also wanted to move to town to get a better education or a job. Men joined their families, but often there was not enough work or the work was not as fulfilling as hunting. More people now live in towns than in rural settlements, but unemployment is a problem.

Even the larger towns are still quite small. Most are built around a harbor or above a fjord. Rocky hills and the ice cap are never far away. Bright-colored houses dot the landscape while rows of apartment buildings rise on the edges of town. Housing is expensive. Construction materials must be imported. Regardless, the towns are growing. Nuuk and other bigger towns offer modern conveniences such as restaurants, galleries, theaters, music venues, and more.

Health Care

The government provides health care for all Greenlanders. There is one hospital in Nuuk and several regional health

A woman consults a doctor over the internet.

Soccer is popular in
Greenland, and is even
played in the snow.

care centers. Smaller villages have a clinic with a nurse. The
health centers provide general care, and basic surgeries can
be performed there. Patients with complicated health needs
are flown to Nuuk by helicopter. "Tele-medicine" is a growing form of patient care. A patient's X-rays and other tests are
sometimes emailed to doctors, who can treat the patients long
distance over the internet.

Sports

Greenlanders play many different sports, both outside and
inside. Outdoors, they enjoy soccer, skiing, skating, kayaking,
sledding, snowmobiling, and golf (including ice golf). Soccer
is the most popular sport to both play and watch. Greenland

has several professional teams. Cross-country, or Nordic, skiing is also popular. Greenland is home to some of the world's most challenging Nordic-ski races. The best known is the 100-mile-long (160 km) Arctic Circle Race.

In 2016, Nuuk hosted the Arctic Winter Games, which feature both indoor and outdoor sports. The games include gymnastics and basketball as well as snowshoeing, Nordic skiing, ice hockey, and traditional Arctic games. These traditional games have their roots in hunting skills and include challenges such as the pole push and the sledge jump.

Some people travel to Greenland to take part in extended cross-country ski trips across the frozen wilderness.

One-Foot High Kick

Young people in Greenland enjoy playing cards, video games, and dice, but they also enjoy traditional games of athleticism and skill. One such game is called One-Foot High Kick. To play this game, a target, (traditionally a piece of fur or bone) is suspended at a height chosen by the players. The first player begins by standing near the target with both feet together. The object is to jump and kick the target with one foot and land on the same foot. After each player kicks, the target is raised. Players who miss the target or land on the wrong foot are out. Rounds continue until only one player remains.

The best athletes can top 9 feet (2.7 m) in the one-foot high kick.

Long, dark winters are broken up by Greenlanders playing indoor sports such as handball, table tennis, badminton, and volleyball, and participating in martial arts such as tae kwon do.

Clothing

Greenlanders dress to be comfortable in the cold climate. Traditional clothing was made for working outdoors. Warm, waterproof parkas, anoraks, belts, leggings, and boots were constructed from sealskin, reindeer hide, fur, musk ox wool, and other natural materials. Today, hunters in the remote north wear clothing made of animal hides and fur combined

The National Costume

The national costume is a blend of traditional ceremonial clothing with modern fabrics and designs. The blend of old and new is an important statement of Greenlandic identity and the people's drive for independence. People dress in this style for weddings, festivals, holidays, and other special events.

Women wear embroidered blouses or colorful sweaters made from *quiviut* (musk ox wool). A wide collar called a *nuilarmiut* is worn on top of the sweater or blouse. The earliest nuilarmiuts were made of tiny bone beads. When the Danish arrived, they traded glass beads with the native people. Since then, most nuilarmiuts are made of colorful glass beads.

Both men and women wear a braided sealskin belt, called an *avittat*, and leggings. Men and women wear thigh-high sealskin

A single nuilarmiut can contain as many as sixty-five thousand beads.

boots called *kamiks*. Kamiks are lined with fur from ermine, Arctic hare, or polar bear and are decorated with beads and embroidery. Men also wear dark wool or sealskin leggings and a light-colored anorak.

with new, lightweight and waterproof fabrics. In town, most people live and work in heated buildings and wear Western-style clothing. They wear business attire, jeans, sweaters, and sometimes high fashion. When Greenlanders dress for special occasions, they often wear traditional clothing.

Holidays and Festivals

Most Greenlandic holidays are religious. Christmas is the biggest holiday. People string up lights and place stars in their windows. Families gather to enjoy holiday foods and games. People give gifts and decorate Christmas trees. Because trees

National Holidays

New Year's Day	January 1
Epiphany	January 6
Easter	March/April
General Prayer Day	April/May (Fourth Friday after Easter)
National Day	June 21
Christmas	December 25
Boxing Day	December 26

St. Lucia's Day, a traditional Scandinavian festival that marks the beginning of the Christmas season, is celebrated in Greenland. Children wear white costumes and carry candles.

are scarce in Greenland, Christmas trees are imported from Denmark. New Year's is celebrated much the same as in other European countries, with parties and fireworks. But Greenlanders

celebrate twice—first when it is midnight in Denmark, and four hours later when it is midnight in Greenland. National Day features speeches, parades, folk dancing and folk music, athletic competitions, and special foods.

Food

A traditional Greenlandic diet is mainly seafood and meat. Few fruits and vegetables are grown locally, so people must rely on expensive imports. Stores in towns have a variety of imported goods, including European cheeses, fruits, and breads, along with snacks and fast foods. Some ranchers in the south raise sheep and reindeer for food, but most people eat wild game—musk ox, reindeer, fox, hare, and polar bear,

Whale meat is an Inuit specialty.

A Greenlander harvests vegetables from his garden. Vegetables are becoming more common in Greenland. Some are grown outside during the short growing season and others are grown in greenhouses.

as well as seal, whale, and walrus. Game birds are also a part of the national diet; ptarmigan is a favorite. Greenland's halibut, cod, shrimp, and snow crab are prized around the world, yet in Greenland, seafood is an everyday, ordinary meal.

Today, many people, especially in Nuuk, are expanding their food choices beyond traditional fare. People are eating more local, cold-weather vegetables such as spinach or broccoli and onions. Stores throughout the country are beginning to stock frozen fruits and vegetables, which can be eaten year-round. The government has new programs to serve healthier foods in schools.

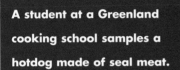

A student at a Greenland cooking school samples a hotdog made of seal meat.

Greenland's Food Ambassador

Anne Sofie Hardenberg is bringing Greenlandic food to the world. Hardenberg is of both Inuit and Danish descent and was raised by her grandmother, who taught her how to cook. Traditional Greenlandic foods are simple. Meat and fish are boiled, dried, grilled, pickled, or eaten raw. Hardenberg shares her love of Greenland's foods in books and cooking classes. She has become Greenland's food ambassador.

She considers Greenland's organic wild meat and fresh seafood the best in the world. Traditional recipes should be protected, she says, but she encourages people to cook in new ways, using native-grown Greenlandic herbs, plants, and edible flowers. Hardenberg frequently attends international food festivals to promote Greenlandic cuisine. One of her specialties is slow-roasted seal seasoned with Arctic thyme.

New and Old

The people of Greenland have a heritage of close family and community life. Whether in town or country, people share common values. The country is building more connections to the outside world through science, trade, tourism, fisheries, and mining. Despite change, the old ways live in people's hearts and continue to inform their behavior and beliefs.

Timeline

Greenland History

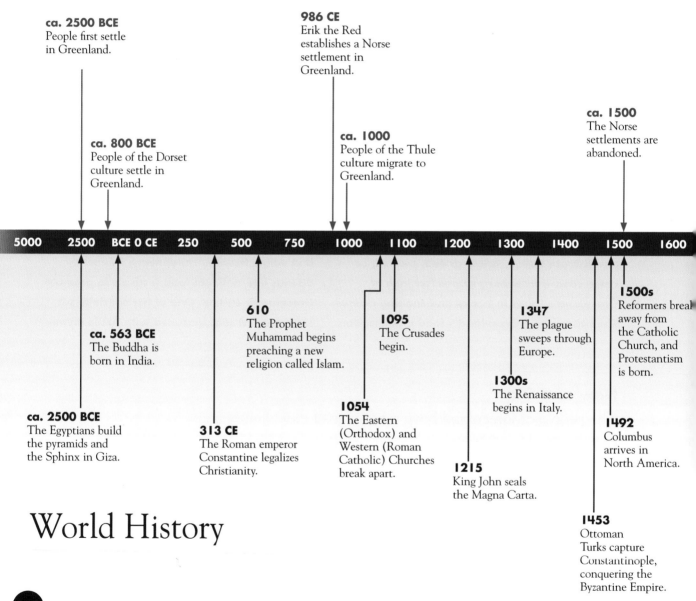

ca. 2500 BCE
People first settle in Greenland.

ca. 800 BCE
People of the Dorset culture settle in Greenland.

986 CE
Erik the Red establishes a Norse settlement in Greenland.

ca. 1000
People of the Thule culture migrate to Greenland.

ca. 1500
The Norse settlements are abandoned.

| 5000 | 2500 | BCE 0 CE | 250 | 500 | 750 | 1000 | 1100 | 1200 | 1300 | 1400 | 1500 | 1600 |

ca. 2500 BCE
The Egyptians build the pyramids and the Sphinx in Giza.

ca. 563 BCE
The Buddha is born in India.

313 CE
The Roman emperor Constantine legalizes Christianity.

610
The Prophet Muhammad begins preaching a new religion called Islam.

1054
The Eastern (Orthodox) and Western (Roman Catholic) Churches break apart.

1095
The Crusades begin.

1215
King John seals the Magna Carta.

1300s
The Renaissance begins in Italy.

1347
The plague sweeps through Europe.

1453
Ottoman Turks capture Constantinople, conquering the Byzantine Empire.

1492
Columbus arrives in North America.

1500s
Reformers break away from the Catholic Church, and Protestantism is born.

World History

1979
Greenland passes Home Rule and establishes a legislature.

1721
Hans Egede begins the Danish colonization of Greenland.

1912
Knud Rasmussen crosses Greenland's ice cap.

2012
Ilulissat glacier calves the largest iceberg ever recorded.

1861
Greenland's first newspaper, *Atuagagdliutit*, is published.

1941
U.S. forces begin occupation of Greenland during World War II.

1989
Summit Station is established.

2009
The Self-Government Act is passed; Greenlandic, or Kalaallisut, is declared the official language.

2016
Nuuk hosts the Arctic Winter Games.

1776
Denmark closes Greenland to foreign trade.

1908-1909
Robert Peary and Matthew Henson travel from Greenland to the North Pole.

1945
Greenland is returned to Denmark.

1700	1800	1900	1920	1940	1960	1980	2000	2005	2010	2015	2020

1945
World War II ends.

2008
The United States elects its first African American president.

1789
The French Revolution begins.

1917
The Bolshevik Revolution brings communism to Russia.

1989
The Berlin Wall is torn down as communism crumbles in Eastern Europe.

1939
World War II begins.

1865
The American Civil War ends.

2004
A tsunami in the Indian Ocean destroys coastlines in Africa, India, and Southeast Asia.

1914
World War I begins.

1991
The Soviet Union breaks into separate states.

1929
A worldwide economic depression begins.

1776
The U.S. Declaration of Independence is signed.

1879
The first practical lightbulb is invented.

1975
The Vietnam War ends.

2016
Donald Trump is elected U.S. president.

2001
Terrorists attack the World Trade Center in New York City and the Pentagon near Washington, D.C.

1969
Humans land on the Moon.

Fast Facts

Official name:	Greenland
Local name:	Kalaallit Nunaat
Capital:	Nuuk
Anthem:	*"Nunarput utoqqarsuanngoravit"* ("You, Our Ancient Land")
Official languages:	Greenlandic (Kalaallisut) and Danish
Type of government:	Parliamentary democracy
Head of state:	Danish monarch
Head of government:	Premier

Left to right: **National flag, voting**

Iceberg in Disko Bay

Latitude and longitude of Nuuk:	64°11' N / 51°43' W
Area:	836,330 square miles (2,166,085 sq km)
Area of ice cap:	656,000 square miles (1.7 million sq km)
Bordering bodies of water:	Arctic Ocean, Greenland Sea, North Atlantic, Nares Strait, Smith Sound, Baffin Bay, Davis Strait
Highest point:	Gunnbjorn Fjeld, 12,119 feet (3,694 m) above sea level
Lowest point:	Sea level along the coast
Longest fjord:	Ittoqqortoormiit Fjord, 217 miles (350 km)
Northernmost point:	Kaffeklubben Island
Average temperature in winter:	About 20°F (–7°C) in the south, –30°F (–34°C) in the north
Average temperature in summer:	About 45°F (7°C) in the south, 40°F (4°C) in the north
Average precipitation North Greenland:	10 inches (25 cm)
Average precipitation South Greenland:	30 inches (76 cm)

National population (2017 est.):	56,171	
Population of major cities (2017 est.):	Nuuk	17,635
	Sisimiut	5,483
	Ilulissat	4,603
	Qaqortoq	3,100
	Aasiaat	3,010

Landmarks:
- ▶ *Aasiaat hot springs,* Aasiaat
- ▶ *Greenland National Museum,* Nuuk
- ▶ *Hvalsey Church,* Qaqortoq
- ▶ *Ittoqqortoormiit Fjord,* Eastern Greenland
- ▶ *Jakobshavn Glacier,* Ilulissat

Economy: Greenland's economy relies on exports of shrimp, halibut, and other fish. They make up 90 percent of total exports. Livestock raising, particularly sheep, is the main form of agriculture in Greenland. Other activities include fish processing, mining, tourism, handicrafts, and harbor and ship maintenance. Denmark provides a subsidy equaling 25 percent of the total value of the goods and services produced in Greenland.

Currency: Danish krone. In 2018, 1 krone equaled $0.16, and $1.00 equaled 6.27 kroner.

System of weights and measures: Metric system

Literacy rate: 100%

Common Greenlandic and Danish words and phrases:

English	Greenlandic	Danish
Hi!	*Aluu!*	*Hej!*
How are you?	*Qanoq ippit?*	*Hvordan har du/de det?*
I am well.	*Ajunngilanga*	*Jeg har det fint, tak.*
Good-bye	*Ajunnginniarna*	*Farvel*
Please	*Ikinngutinnersumik*	*Hvis du vil vaere sa venlig at*
Thank you	*Qujanarsuaq*	*Mange tak*

Prominent Greenlanders: Hans Egede   (1686–1758)
Norwegian missionary

Hans Lynge   (1906–1988)
Author, artist

Sofie Petersen   (1955–)
First female bishop of Greenland

Knud Rasmussen   (1879–1933)
Inuit explorer, social scientist, author

Erik Thorvaldsson (Erik the Red)   (ca. 950–ca. 1003)
Viking explorer

Clockwise from top: **Currency, Knud Rasmussen, schoolchildren**

To Find Out More

Books

▶ *Investigating Earth's Polar Biomes*. New York: Britannica Educational Publishers, 2012.

▶ Kallen, Stuart A. *Native Peoples of the Arctic*. Minneapolis: Lerner Publications, 2017.

▶ Royston, Angela. *What Happens When an Ice Cap Melts?* Mankato, MN: Smart Apple Media, 2016.

▶ Weil, Ann. *The World's Most Amazing National Parks*. Chicago: Raintree, 2012.

Video

▶ *Chasing Ice*. Boulder, CO: Exposure Labs, 2012.

▶ *Greenland: A Vast, Unknown Land*. Animal Planet, 2015.

▶ *Why Is Greenland Melting?* Frontline PBS, Public Broadcasting System, 2017.

▶ Visit this Scholastic website for more information on Greenland:
www.factsfornow.scholastic.com
Enter the keyword **Greenland**

Index

Page numbers in *italics* indicate illustrations.

Meet the Author

Ruth Bjorklund grew up in rural New England where she went hiking, rowing, and sailing. She left New England, traveled, and eventually settled in Seattle, Washington, where she attended the University of Washington. There, she earned a bachelor's degree in comparative literature and a master's degree in library and information science.

She has been a children's and young adult librarian and has written many books on a wide range of subjects, including the history, geography, and culture of states and countries, health, endangered animals, and contemporary issues.

Today, Bjorklund lives on Bainbridge Island, a ferry ride away from Seattle. She enjoys kayaking, sailing, camping, and traveling.

Photo Credits